Learning jqPlot

Learn how to create your very own rich and intuitive
JavaScript data visualizations using jqPlot

Scott Gottreu

open source*

community experience distilled

PUBLISHING

BIRMINGHAM - MUMBAI

Learning jqPlot

Copyright © 2014 Packt Publishing

First published: August 2014

Production reference: 1200814

Published by Packt Publishing Ltd.
Livery Place
35 Livery Street
Birmingham B3 2PB, UK.

ISBN 978-1-78398-116-8

www.packtpub.com

Cover image by Manu Gangadhar (manug30@gmail.com)

Credits

Author

Scott Gottreu

Reviewers

Hrishikesh Choudhari

Chris Leonello

Alex Libby

Mihir Mone

Anirudh Prabhu

Taroon Tyagi

Commissioning Editor

Kartikey Pandey

Acquisition Editor

Richard Harvey

Content Development Editor

Balaji Naidu

Technical Editors

Manal Pednekar

Akash Rajiv Sharma

Ankita Thakur

Copy Editors

Sayanee Mukherjee

Laxmi Subramanian

Project Coordinators

Judie Jose

Aaron S. Lazar

Proofreaders

Simran Bhogal

Maria Gould

Ameesha Green

Indexers

Hemangini Bari

Mariammal Chettiyar

Rekha Nair

Priya Subramani

Graphics

Ronak Dhruv

Production Coordinator

Arvindkumar Gupta

Cover Work

Arvindkumar Gupta

About the Author

Scott Gottreu has worked across a range of industries; academic, medical, advertising, nonprofit, and private sector organizations. Each time, he expanded his knowledge base while solving problems specific to that sector. He started off in classic ASP and moved on to PHP, and is now using Rails as well. He learned JavaScript and jQuery along the way.

He currently works for Warren Douglas Advertising in Fort Worth, Texas, where he creates solutions for his company's various clients.

I would like to thank my co-workers for being a sounding board, while I worked out the examples for this book. A big thank you to my boss, Doug Briley, for giving me the freedom to work on this book during company time. Finally, to my friends and family, you deserve a big thank you as well, for listening to my fears and being supportive and encouraging.

About the Reviewers

Hrishikesh Choudhari has been developing single-page rich applications using a host of client-side technologies. He has a special preference for JSON-emitting servers and popular interfaces on the frontend. He has worked on the backend for innovative social networks.

He is a professional data visualization expert, and he builds his own visualization microlibraries for SVG. He has also contributed to *FusionCharts Beginner's Guide*, *Packt Publishing*. He helped design dashboards for clients ranging from Fortune 10 companies to start-ups.

He works on his skills to be a full stack web architect. He graduated Magna Cum Laude in B.S. in Software Engineering from Champlain College, USA.

In his free time, he speed-reads, cooks, and goes for long walks. You can follow him on Twitter at `@hchoudhari` or on LinkedIn at `https://linkedin.com/in/hrishikeshchoudhari`. His website is `http://hrishikeshchoudhari.com/`.

Chris Leonello has been programming for over 30 years. He began web programming in 1996, developing websites and remote data monitoring systems in HTML and Java. He has experience with programming languages from Awk to XSLT, but prefers to work in Python and JavaScript. He is also well-versed in database design and administration.

Chris works as an engineer, developing and running computer simulations. He also creates systems to store, mine, and visualize data. He became active in the open source community in 2009, when, needing a browser-based chart that allowed client-side data manipulation with automatically updating trend lines, he created jqPlot.

Although this is the first book he has been invited to review, he enjoys helping people learn. In the past, he has taught courses on HTML, networking, and Internet standards. When not working, he enjoys making his kids laugh, running, bicycling, and watching movies.

Alex Libby works in IT support. He has been involved in supporting end users for the last 15 years in a variety of different environments. He currently works as a technical analyst, supporting a medium-sized SharePoint estate for a global parts distributor based in the U.K. Although he gets to play with different technologies in his day job, his first true love has always been with the open source movement, and in particular, experimenting with CSS3, HTML5, and jQuery. To date, he has worked on a number of books for Packt Publishing, including *HTML5 Video How-To*, *jQuery Tools UI Library*, and *jQuery UI 1.10: The User Interface Library for jQuery*.

Mihir Mone is a postgraduate from Monash University, Australia. Although he did his postgraduation in Network Computing, he mainly does web and mobile development these days.

After spending some time fiddling around with routers and switches, he quickly decided to build upon his passion for web development; not design, but development. Building web systems and applications rather than websites with all the fancy flash animations was something that was very interesting and alluring to him. He even returned to his alma mater to teach all about web development in order to pay forward what he had learned.

These days, he works for a small software/engineering house in Melbourne doing web development and prototyping exciting new ideas in the data visualization and UX domain.

He is also a big JavaScript fan and previously reviewed the book *Instant jQuery Flot Visual Data Analysis*, *Packt Publishing*.

He is a Linux enthusiast and a big proponent of the OSS movement, and believes that software should always be free to actualize its true potential. A true geek at heart, he spends some of his leisure time writing code in the hope that it may be helpful to the masses.

He is also a motorsport junkie, so you may find him loitering around the race tracks from time to time (especially if there is Formula 1 involved).

Anirudh Prabhu is a software engineer at Xoriant Corporation with 4 years of experience in web designing and development. He is responsible for JavaScript development and maintenance in his project. His areas of expertise are HTML, CSS, JavaScript, and jQuery. When not working, Anirudh loves reading, listening to music, and photography.

He did his MSc in Information Technology. He has also reviewed a few titles related to JavaScript and CSS for Packt Publishing and Apress Publications.

Taroon Tyagi is a dreamer, designer, and solution architect. He is a rationalistic optimist, with a lust for food, technology, and knowledge. He has over 5 years of professional and industrial experience in web, UX, and UI design and frontend development. He is currently working as the Head of Design and Interaction at Fizzy Software Pvt. Ltd, based out of Gurgaon, India.

When online, he is constantly involved in the web communities, experimenting with new technologies and looking for inspiration. When offline, he is found enjoying music, books, wireframing, and digging philosophy.

He has worked as a technical reviewer on a few books for Packt Publishing.

www.PacktPub.com

Support files, eBooks, discount offers, and more

You might want to visit www.PacktPub.com for support files and downloads related to your book.

Did you know that Packt offers eBook versions of every book published, with PDF and ePub files available? You can upgrade to the eBook version at www.PacktPub.com and as a print book customer, you are entitled to a discount on the eBook copy. Get in touch with us at service@packtpub.com for more details.

At www.PacktPub.com, you can also read a collection of free technical articles, sign up for a range of free newsletters and receive exclusive discounts and offers on Packt books and eBooks.

http://PacktLib.PacktPub.com

Do you need instant solutions to your IT questions? PacktLib is Packt's online digital book library. Here, you can access, read and search across Packt's entire library of books.

Why subscribe?

- Fully searchable across every book published by Packt
- Copy and paste, print and bookmark content
- On demand and accessible via web browser

Free access for Packt account holders

If you have an account with Packt at www.PacktPub.com, you can use this to access PacktLib today and view nine entirely free books. Simply use your login credentials for immediate access.

Table of Contents

Preface

The term "Big Data" is all over tech news. But what does it really mean? Big Data refers to the problem of trying to process and analyze large amounts of data. Generally, Big Data refers to the petabytes of data, which is over 1 million gigabytes. You are likely to face your own Big Data issues, just on a smaller scale. If you only have one web server, processing or analyzing a database of only one gigabyte can be overwhelming.

Another part of the Big Data problem is the source and format of the data. It is coming from many sources and it's not easy to match all of the data points. You probably have years of transactional data in a MySQL database, as well as APIs to Google Analytics, Facebook, Twitter, and any other services your company uses.

Once you can figure out how to process the data, you need to do something with it. That's where jqPlot comes in. Using charts to display large datasets makes it easier to see trends or correlations in the data. jqPlot allows you to create charts quickly so that you can move on to analyze your data.

Many technical books give examples that don't match anything you might deal with in the real world. I'm writing this book about the various problems we face working in the fictional company jQ Big Box Electronics. We will work through real-world examples that reflect the reality of the "Big Data" world we live in. I hope that placing these examples in a practical context will help you understand the rationale for using a certain chart for a particular dataset and build on the skills you will acquire from this book.

What this book covers

Chapter 1, *Getting Started*, will briefly give an introduction on how to create a jqPlot object and how the plugin handles data. Then, we'll start creating our first charts, as well as looking at different options for formatting lines and marks.

Chapter 2, *More Line Charts, Area Charts, and Scatter Plots*, discusses the different ways in which you can load data into your chart, including using AJAX to a remote service. Then, we'll move on to discussing what area charts and scatter plots are, and their best uses.

Chapter 3, *Bar Charts and Digging into Data*, discusses the best uses of bar charts. We'll also see different options for axis and tick labels including rotatable labels. We'll finish up with clickable data points and will look at how to use these to drill down into more complicated data.

Chapter 4, *Horizontal and Stacked Bar Charts*, teaches you about horizontal and stacked bar charts. We'll also look at axis padding and positioning of data point labels.

Chapter 5, *Pie Charts and Donut Charts*, discusses the specific uses of pie charts and donut charts. We'll also see some specific options for pie charts.

Chapter 6, *Spice Up Your Charts with Animation, Tooltips, and Highlighting*, teaches how to animate your own charts and how to create tooltips. We'll also cover data point highlighting and cursor highlighting.

Chapter 7, *Stock Market Charts – OHLC and Candlestick Charts*, discusses OHLC and candlestick charts, and their specific uses. We'll also learn the method to format the text included in the tooltips.

Chapter 8, *Bubble Charts, Block Plots, and Waterfalls*, looks at some different charts that are heavier on the visualization of data over the representation of the data.

Chapter 9, *Showing Real-time Data with Our Charts*, discusses the methods that allow us to redraw or recreate a given plot after it is has been generated. We'll take this newfound knowledge and see how to update our charts automatically at set intervals.

Chapter 10, *Beautifying and Extending Your Charts*, explains how to create different themes for our plots and the various CSS options available to style our charts.

Chapter 11, *Bringing it All Together*, combines everything you have learned and merges the different chart types into one plot, as well as styling your new charts. You will also see how jqPlot can be extended with the new rendering plugins.

Appendix, *Answers*, helps us find the answers to all the learning questions found throughout the book.

What you need for this book

You use jQuery for most of your projects, so you're well on your way to learning jqPlot. Here's what else you'll need to get up and running with jqPlot:

- Your favorite IDE or text editor. If you don't have a favorite, you can try out Sublime Text, `http://www.sublimetext.com`, for Mac OS, or Notepad++, `http://notepad-plus-plus.org/`, for Windows.

- Your choice of browser. JqPlot will work with IE6 and higher, but needs extra plugins to replicate the canvas functionality found in modern browsers. These additional plugins are included with jqPlot.

- The latest version of jQuery, which is available at `http://jquery.com/download/`. Either Version 2.x or 1.x will work with jqPlot, but if you need support for IE7 or IE8, you will need to use jQuery 1.1x.

- The latest version of jqPlot, which is available at `https://bitbucket.org/cleonello/jqplot/downloads/`.

That's it! You don't need anything else. Ideally, you would incorporate your charts into a larger project such as your company intranet. This would also be the best place to get the data for your charts.

Who this book is for

This book is for everyone who uses jQuery for their projects. More specifically, this book is for everyone who has ever experienced something like the following scenario: "We've got 3 years of data that we need to analyze and chart by Friday. Work your magic."

I'm writing this book to help you solve problems. You're a developer, so you are smart and curious. If you're like me, you like seeing how data is interconnected. So, I want to help you determine the best way to present the data that your boss dumped on you.

As you begin working, I want to help you begin thinking of other data points you could bring into your reports. As you begin thinking of new connections, this will help those who will be looking at the data when you're done. In the end, I want to make you a hero to your boss.

Conventions

In this book, you will find a number of styles of text that distinguish between different kinds of information. Here are some examples of these styles, and an explanation of their meaning.

Code words in text, database table names, folder names, filenames, file extensions, pathnames, dummy URLs, user input, and Twitter handles are shown as follows: "For the `yaxis` option, we set our `label` and use the `formatString` option to format our values as currency."

A block of code is set as follows:

```
<script>
$(document).ready(function(){
   var secondPlot = $.jqplot ('secondChart', [[[5,4],[10,7],[15,6],
[20,9]]]);
   });
</script>
<div id="secondChart" style="width:400px;"></div>
```

When we wish to draw your attention to a particular part of a code block, the relevant lines or items are set in bold:

```
<script src="../js/jqplot.dateAxisRenderer.min.js"></script>
<script>
$(document).ready(function(){

  var revenue = [['2012-07-20', 807403], ['2012-08-20', 755840],
['2012-09-20', 775304]];
  var profit = [['2012-07-20', 193793.82], ['2012-08-20', 183221.56],
['2012-09-20', 192797.31]];
  var electronics = [['2012-07-20', 116276.29], ['2012-08-20',
95867.97], ['2012-09-20', 120591.27]];
  var media = [['2012-07-20', 27596.25], ['2012-08-20', 32396.47],
['2012-09-20', 26709.06]];
  var nerd_corral = [['2012-07-20', 49921.28], ['2012-08-20',
54957.12], ['2012-09-20', 45496.98]];

  var rev_profit = $.jqplot ('division_profit', [revenue, profit,
electronics, media, nerd_corral],
  {
```

New terms and important words are shown in bold. Words that you see on the screen, in menus or dialog boxes for example, appear in the text like this: "We test our chart, and a trend line for **DVDs/Blu-ray** is rendered since we did not pass a query string."

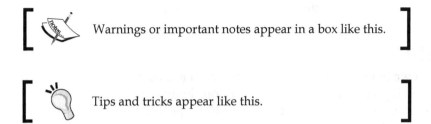

Warnings or important notes appear in a box like this.

Tips and tricks appear like this.

Reader feedback

Feedback from our readers is always welcome. Let us know what you think about this book—what you liked or may have disliked. Reader feedback is important for us to develop titles that you really get the most out of.

To send us general feedback, simply send an e-mail to feedback@packtpub.com, and mention the book title through the subject of your message.

If there is a topic that you have expertise in and you are interested in either writing or contributing to a book, see our author guide on www.packtpub.com/authors.

Customer support

Now that you are the proud owner of a Packt book, we have a number of things to help you to get the most from your purchase.

Downloading the example code

You can download the example code files for all Packt books you have purchased from your account at http://www.packtpub.com. If you purchased this book elsewhere, you can visit http://www.packtpub.com/support and register to have the files e-mailed directly to you.

Downloading the color images of this book

We also provide you a PDF file that has color images of the screenshots/diagrams used in this book. The color images will help you better understand the changes in the output. You can download this file from `https://www.packtpub.com/sites/default/files/downloads/1168OS_ColoredImages.pdf`.

Errata

Although we have taken every care to ensure the accuracy of our content, mistakes do happen. If you find a mistake in one of our books—maybe a mistake in the text or the code—we would be grateful if you would report this to us. By doing so, you can save other readers from frustration and help us improve subsequent versions of this book. If you find any errata, please report them by visiting `http://www.packtpub.com/support`, selecting your book, clicking on the **errata submission form** link, and entering the details of your errata. Once your errata are verified, your submission will be accepted and the errata will be uploaded to our website, or added to any list of existing errata, under the Errata section of that title.

Piracy

Piracy of copyright material on the Internet is an ongoing problem across all media. At Packt, we take the protection of our copyright and licenses very seriously. If you come across any illegal copies of our works, in any form, on the Internet, please provide us with the location address or website name immediately so that we can pursue a remedy.

Please contact us at `copyright@packtpub.com` with a link to the suspected pirated material.

We appreciate your help in protecting our authors, and our ability to bring you valuable content.

Questions

You can contact us at `questions@packtpub.com` if you are having a problem with any aspect of the book, and we will do our best to address it.

1
Getting Started

As we begin this journey, we will look at the advantages of jqPlot over other web-based charting tools. We will look at the basic options available to us in jqPlot as we hit the ground running and create charts based on our company's data. In this chapter, we will cover the following topics:

- Review the components of a chart
- Learn the different ways of creating a chart in jqPlot
- Create arrays that contain values for our x and y axes and pass these into jqPlot
- Use a plugin that allows us to use dates for our x axis
- Create multiple lines on our chart
- Add multiple y axes to our chart
- Add a legend to one of our charts
- Set different options for our lines and use different marker options

Reviewing the components of a chart

Let's think back to our high school Math class where our teacher discussed charts and graphs. You might have been like me and wondered how you would apply this in real life. Fast forward to today and your boss dropping a stack of files on your desk just made it real.

We will use line charts as a basis for our review of the parts of a chart. Line charts are one of the most popular charts to use, while also being the simplest to understand and implement with jqPlot. Line charts are mainly used to show how data changes over time, but they can also be used to show how one dataset impacts another. For example, we can show how the number of social media shares affect revenue or how sales in different divisions affect the gross profit margin.

With this in mind, we need to look at the components of a chart. There are two axes, the *x* axis and the *y* axis. Some might think of these as independent variables and dependent variables, but they are more scientific labels. An easier way to think of the two axes would be cause and effect. Our *y* axis generally represents the dependent variable or effect, which for instance, can be the amount of profit generated during a given time period, or the total revenue generated by a sales associate.

Our *x* axis generally represents the independent variable or cause. Most line charts show trending data over time, where our *x* axis covers certain time frames such as days, weeks, or years. Usually, we have a set range of data points on our *x* axis, as a result of which our *y* axis will have data points that may vary greatly. If we had a chart showing the revenue generated by sales associates, their names would be on the *x* axis. The sales associates interact with the customers and generate the sales that provide the revenue.

A few other pieces of a chart to keep in mind are the grid and ticks. The ticks denote certain values along the axis. The grid represents the lines running vertically and horizontally, connecting the ticks on both axes. The grid makes it easier to decipher the value of each point of a line on the chart. The following diagram shows how each of these pieces composes a chart:

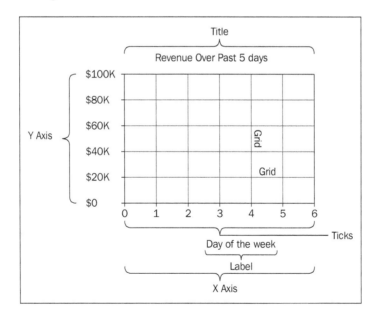

Getting a promotion

Calvin, our boss, stops by our office and informs us that all the regional managers will be coming to the corporate offices for a quarterly meeting on Friday. Since it is Monday, we should be able to meet this goal. He wants us to create a few pages for our intranet, showing things such as profit, revenue, and expenses.

"We've got to impress them," he says as he leaves. We stare at each other, simply bewildered. You mention that we just became business analysts as well as developers.

We start to work in our newfound roles. You begin to find the data that will be required. Since we are creating prototypes, we need to manually compile the data for now.

I start researching web-based charting tools and come across three main contenders: Highcharts, D3.js, and jqPlot. We will have to pay a licensing fee to use Highcharts for our company. D3.js has a beautiful gallery of available charts, and it looks like it has a very high learning curve. It appears that jqPlot has a lower learning curve and we will be building charts faster with jqPlot than with D3.js. The other benefit of jqPlot is that it does not require a commercial license.

Creating a jqPlot chart

Download the current version of jqPlot and extract the files to your web server. We'll create the most basic chart we can, as shown in the following steps:

1. We start by building our HTML file, including jQuery. We also include the jqPlot JavaScript and CSS files from the downloaded ZIP file. We must include jQuery because jqPlot is a plugin for jQuery, which means that it needs jQuery to function properly:

```
<!doctype html>
   <head>
     <title>Learning jqPlot</title>
     <meta charset="utf-8">
     <link rel="stylesheet" href="/css/jquery.jqplot.min.css">
    <script src="../js/jquery.min.js"></script>
     <script src="../js/jquery.jqplot.min.js"></script>
   </head>
   <body>
```

2. Next, we create the div element that will contain our chart. We set id to firstChart so that jqPlot will know where to build our chart. Since we are just creating prototypes, we will set the width of our div inline, as shown in the following code.

```
<div id="firstChart" style="width:600px"></div>
```

3. Finally, we create our jqPlot object and store it in the plot variable. Then, we pass the id attribute of the div, which is firstChart. Finally, we include an array of numbers inside another array, which will be our data points. This is the simplest way to pass in the data:

```
<script>
$(document).ready(function(){
    var plot = $.jqplot ('firstChart', [[1,9,4,3,8,5]]);
});
</script>
</body>
</html>
```

We can also create our chart by chaining the jqPlot plugin to the jQuery selector of our div. It will look like the following:

```
$("#firstChart").jqplot ([[1,9,4,3,8,5]]);
```

In our examples, we will store our objects in variables so that they are available globally in our JavaScript if required.

jqPlot will interpret each number as a point on the *y* axis, and it will assign a value for the *x* axis, starting with 1. We can see the result of our effort in the following screenshot:

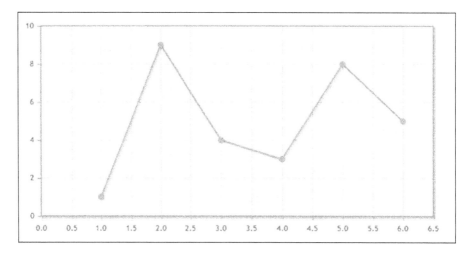

Passing in both x and y values

The next option to pass in data to the chart is to use a two-dimensional array. Our inner array contains individual arrays, which in turn contain the value for *x* axis followed by the value for *y* axis. When we include both *x* and *y* values, our data points may not increment at a constant interval, as was the case in our previous chart:

```
<script>
$(document).ready(function(){
    var secondPlot = $.jqplot ('secondChart', [[[5,4],[10,7],[15,6],
[20,9]]]);
});
</script>
<div id="secondChart" style="width:400px;"></div>
```

We load this new chart in our web browser, and the results are as shown in the following figure:

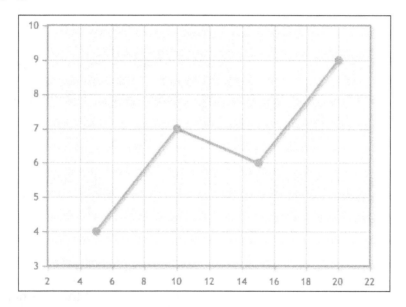

Using dates for the x axis

As we finish our first experiment, you mention that you've found the revenue numbers for the last 7 days. We decide that it will be best if we can show the dates on the *x* axis and not use arbitrary numbers.

We will need to make use of one of the renderers available in jqPlot. A renderer extends the basic functionality of jqPlot. Some renderers take the data and render it in different chart types. Other renderers format text in different ways. For our next chart, we will use `dateAxisRenderer`, which will take our human-readable dates and convert them into values for jqPlot to render:

1. We start by including the `dateAxisRenderer.js` file in our HTML, as shown in the following code:

    ```
    <script src="../js/jqplot.dateAxisRenderer.min.js"></script>
    ```

2. To make it easier to keep track of our data, we will store it in an array and then pass that variable into our plot. Our array contains arrays with the x and y values for each data point. The date is the x value, and the second number is our y value:

    ```
    <script>
    $(document).ready(function(){
        var revenue = [['2012-10-25',258142], ['2012-10-
    26',267924],['2012-10-27',239140], ['2012-10-28',230107], ['2012-
    10-29',264397], ['2012-10-30',276369], ['2012-10-31',285050]];
    ```

3. Next, we declare the variable for our chart. We pass in the ID of the div, and then pass in the `revenue` array. No matter how many data arrays we create, they will all be housed inside another array. We also want to set some options for our chart. This is accomplished by passing a jQuery object as the third parameter:

    ```
    var revenuePlot = $.jqplot ('revenueChart', [revenue],
        {
    ```

4. After creating the object, we set the `title` option and then create an object for our axes:

    ```
    title:'Daily Revenue',
    axes:{
    ```

5. We set the `renderer` option for the *x* axis. We will pass in the `DateAxisRenderer` class. Since it is a class, we will not place it inside quotes. Also, we will not add parentheses to the end of the class name. This will instantiate our class:

    ```
    xaxis:{
      renderer:$.jqplot.DateAxisRenderer,
      label: 'Days of the Month'
    },
    ```

6. For the `yaxis` option, we set our `label` and use the `formatString` option to format our values as currency. The dollar sign in `formatString` adds a dollar sign to the beginning of the tick. The apostrophe states we want a thousands place separator. Finally, the `d` expression tells jqPlot to treat the tick as a number. We complete the page by including the div element to contain our chart:

```
                yaxis:{
                    label: 'Revenue in Dollars',
                    tickOptions: { formatString: "$%'d" }
                }
            }
        });
    });
</script>
<div id="revenueChart" style="width:600px;"></div>
```

 Because of issues with time zones and how browsers calculate dates, it's best to include a time along with the date. The date renderer will also accept epoch timestamps. We need to keep in mind that if a time zone is not included in our date string, JavaScript will default to the time zone of the browser.

With our new chart complete, we load the page in our browser and see the result in the following figure:

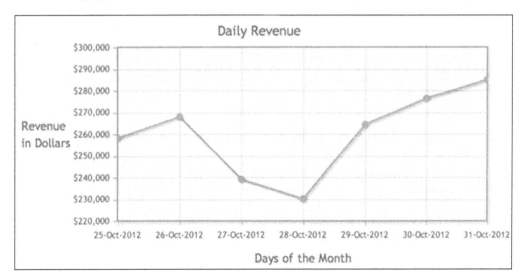

Adding multiple data series

This is a nice start, but we both agree that the leadership is going to want more than just a couple of days of revenue on a chart. Our next chart will display the profit and revenue numbers for the last 12 months. We will only need to make a few adjustments to our previous chart:

1. We include both arrays containing our revenue and profit figures:

```
<script src="../js/jqplot.dateAxisRenderer.min.js"></script>

<script>
$(document).ready(function(){

  var revenue = [['2011-11-20', 800538], ['2011-12-20', 804879],
  ['2012-01-20', 847732], ['2012-02-20', 795758], ['2012-03-20',
  835554], ['2012-04-20', 844379], ['2012-05-20', 828510], ['2012-
  06-20', 753984], ['2012-07-20', 807403], ['2012-08-20', 755840],
  ['2012-09-20', 775304], ['2012-10-20', 781322]];

  var profit = [['2011-11-20', 192049.56], ['2011-12-20',
  188744.75], ['2012-01-20', 197352.54], ['2012-02-20', 190106.74],
  ['2012-03-20', 193453.07], ['2012-04-20', 197249.69], ['2012-
  05-20', 205480.18], ['2012-06-20', 177648.78], ['2012-07-20',
  193793.82], ['2012-08-20', 183221.56], ['2012-09-20', 192797.31],
  ['2012-10-20', 182451.68]];
```

2. We modify the variable name for our object and create a new ID attribute. Next, we combine both arrays into a container array and pass it into jqPlot. Within jqPlot, each array containing data is called a series and both series will appear on the same *y* axis:

```
  var rev_profit = $.jqplot ('revenueProfitChart', [revenue,
profit],
  {
```

3. We modify the title and the labels for our axes. We also update the ID of our div element:

```
    title:'Monthly Revenue & Profit',
    axes:{
      xaxis:{
        renderer:$.jqplot.DateAxisRenderer,
        label: 'Months'
      },
      yaxis:{
        label: 'Totals Dollars',
        tickOptions: { formatString: "$%'d" }
```

```
        }
      }
    });
  });
</script>
<div id="revenueProfitChart" style="width:600px;"></div>
```

We load the page in the browser and smile. The changes to the chart get us closer to what the management is looking for. We can see the results of our efforts in the following figure.

Adding multiple y axes

The two data series are really far apart in their values. It's hard to decipher the value of each point by just looking at the chart. We'll put each series on its own *y* axis. This will make it easier to see interactions between our revenue and profit. We revisit the code and begin to alter it to separate the *y* axes.

1. We start by adding the `series` option. It is an array containing an object for each data series. For the first series, we can leave the default settings in place. So, we simply pass in an empty object. The second series will be on the second *y* axis, which means that we enter `y2axis` for the `yaxis` option. The ticks and label for this axis will appear on the right-hand side of our chart:

    ```
    var rev_profit = $.jqplot ('revenueProfitChart', [revenue,
    profit],
      {
        title:'Monthly Revenue & Profit',
    ```

```
series:[
  {},
  {yaxis:'y2axis'}
],
```

2. We change the label for `yaxis` to `Revenue`. We copy all these options for `y2axis`. We then change the axis option and the label:

```
axes:{
  xaxis:{
    renderer:$.jqplot.DateAxisRenderer,
    label: 'Months'
  },
  yaxis:{
    label: 'Revenue',
    tickOptions: { formatString: "$%'d" }
  },
  y2axis:{
    label: 'Profit',
    tickOptions: { formatString: "$%'d" }
  }
}
});
```

We load this new chart in our browser. The fruit of our labors can be seen in the following figure:

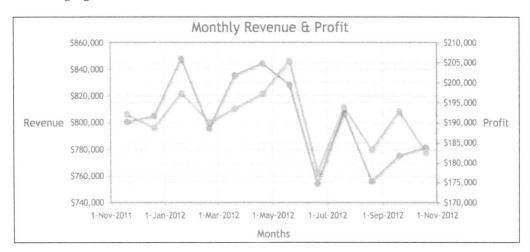

We begin to study the chart. It appears that profit as a part of revenue is better in some months when compared to other months, but we can't draw any clear conclusions from this chart. However, this can be a springboard to try to track down some correlations.

Adding a legend

As we study the chart, we lose track of which line represents revenue and which represents profit. We'll need a legend to solve this problem:

1. We start by adding labels to each of our series objects. We add a `label` object to our empty object for the first data series. For the second series, we add the `label` option alongside the existing `yaxis` option.

    ```
    title:'Monthly Revenue & Profit',
    series:[
      { label: 'Revenue' },
      { label: 'Profit', yaxis:'y2axis' }
    ],
    ```

2. Next, we add a `legend` option. In order for the legend to appear, we must set the `show` option to `true`. We also set placement to `outsideGrid`. The other two options available to us are `insideGrid` and `outside`. The `outsideGrid` option will place the legend outside the grid, but inside the plot object. Hence, the grid will be resized to accommodate the legend:

    ```
    legend: {
      show: true,
      placement: 'outsideGrid'
    },
    ```

We finish the updates to our new chart and open our web browser again. We now have a legend that will help us decipher our chart, which can be seen in the following figure:

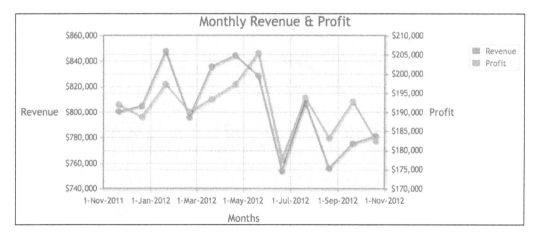

The insideGrid option will place the legend inside the grid. If we want the legend outside the grid, but we don't want our grid to shrink, we can use the outside option instead. Be aware that with the outside option, our legend can flow outside the plot and overlap other elements on our page.

We finally have a nice report. We call Calvin and ask him to come by and take a look at what we've got so far. We also need some direction on how to proceed. A few minutes later, he swings by our office.

"This is great," he says, "but we're going to need to expand on some of this data. How about we get a report that has last quarter's revenue and break out the profit by each division? Also, can you change the styles on those lines? Add a little flair or something." Calvin walks out and we stare at each other, trying to figure out how to add some "flair" to our report.

Adding line and marker options

We'll keep the first two data series as they are and put all the divisional data on y3axis. You mention that we can use different marker styles to set off the different divisions. We will turn off the line for the revenue and overall profit data series and just show the markers. As for the divisional series, we've got seven different styles to use for our markers, which are the following:

- circle and filledCircle
- diamond and filledDiamond
- square and filledSquare
- x

This works out well because we've got three major divisions in our data. You find the profit numbers that we will need, and we set to work updating our chart.

1. We start by including the profit numbers for each division. We also pass the following three data series arrays in to jqPlot:

```
<script src="../js/jqplot.dateAxisRenderer.min.js"></script>
<script>
$(document).ready(function(){

  var revenue = [['2012-07-20', 807403], ['2012-08-20', 755840],
['2012-09-20', 775304]];
  var profit = [['2012-07-20', 193793.82], ['2012-08-20',
183221.56], ['2012-09-20', 192797.31]];
```

```
   var electronics = [['2012-07-20', 116276.29], ['2012-08-20',
95867.97], ['2012-09-20', 120591.27]];
   var media = [['2012-07-20', 27596.25], ['2012-08-20', 32396.47],
['2012-09-20', 26709.06]];
   var nerd_corral = [['2012-07-20', 49921.28], ['2012-08-20',
54957.12], ['2012-09-20', 45496.98]];

   var rev_profit = $.jqplot ('division_profit', [revenue, profit,
electronics, media, nerd_corral],
   {
```

2. Now that we have five series across three different axes, we will make use of the `seriesDefaults` option. By setting `yaxis` to `y3axis`, every data series will appear on this axis unless we override this option on the individual series. We also set the `style` option to `filledCircle`:

```
title:'Q3 Revenue, Profit & Divisional Profits',
seriesDefaults: {
  yaxis:'y3axis',
  markerOptions: {
    style: 'filledCircle',
    size: 10
  }
},
```

3. Next, we create the `series` objects for revenue and profit. We set the `showLine` option to `false` along with `style` for `markerOptions`. Since we set the default axis in `seriesDefaults`, we also need to override this option:

```
series:[
  {
    label: 'Revenue',
    yaxis:'yaxis',
    showLine: false,
    markerOptions: { style: 'x' }
  },
  {
    label: 'Profit',
    yaxis:'y2axis',
    showLine: false,
    markerOptions: { style: 'diamond' }
  },
```

4. For the `Electronics` division data series, we use the defaults. For the two remaining series, we set the `style` option to different values:

```
{ label: 'Electronics' },
{
  label: 'Media & Software',
  markerOptions: { style: 'filledSquare' }
},
{
  label: 'Nerd Corral',
  markerOptions: { style: 'filledDiamond' }
}
],
```

5. Our next step is to set the default options under `axesDefaults`. We set the default `formatString` for currency, but this will cause problems for our *x* axis:

```
axesDefaults: {
  tickOptions: { formatString: "$%'d" }
},
```

6. Since we use the date renderer, we set the `formatString` option of the *x* axis to `%B`, which will output the full month name as the tick. jqPlot automatically calculates how many ticks it thinks we need for our axes. However, jqPlot sometimes creates more than we need. Since this chart deals with quarterly data, we set `numberTicks` to 3:

```
axes:{
  xaxis:{
    label: 'Months',
    renderer:$.jqplot.DateAxisRenderer,
    numberTicks: 3,
    tickOptions: { formatString: "%B" }
  },
  yaxis: { label: 'Revenue' },
  y2axis: { label: 'Profit' }
}
});
});
</script>
```

7. With the added axis for our chart, we need to increase the width of our div.

```
<div id="division_profit" style="width:650px;"></div>
```

It was hard keeping track of all these options. We open our web browser, hoping we did everything correctly. We can see the result in the following figure. All the axes have different values. The lines for revenue and profit are missing, just as we wanted, and each data series has a different marker.

Everything worked as we intended, but the chart is hard to read. With the different axes, data points are overlapping. As we continue our research, we might find a better way to represent the same data.

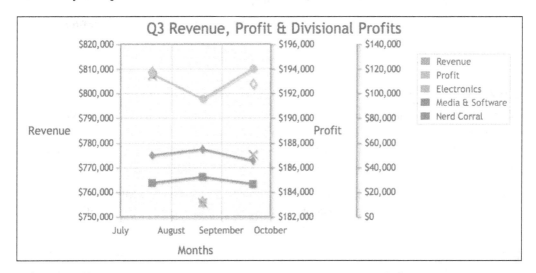

 Since our data points are in the middle of the month, jqPlot will add a month to the end of the x axis to keep everything in bounds. If we only want the three months on the graph, we can change the dates to the first of the month.

Calvin stops by later and loves what we have. "This is a great first step. We will need some charts that pull in data from other sources, especially our social media accounts. We will also need to start showing trend lines."

Calvin walks out again without warning, leaving us to stare at each other. We decide we've done what we can for the morning, so we head off to lunch, preparing ourselves to tackle social media and trend lines upon our return.

Learning questions

1. What are the three main parts of a chart discussed in the chapter?

2. What are the two ways we can create a jqPlot object?

3. How do we enable a data series to appear on the second y axis?

4. What are the three placement options for our legend?

5. What are the four main marker styles?

6. What values do we set for the `formatString` option to get a dollar sign and the thousands place separator?

Summary

We started the chapter by taking a refresher course on the parts of a chart. Next, we learned the advantages of jqPlot and created our first chart with just a few lines of code. Later, we looked at the different ways to pass in data to jqPlot. We made use of `DateAxisRenderer` to use dates on the x axis of our charts.

We learned about options such as `y2axis`, which allowed us to plot our lines on different y axes. We also made use of the `legend` and `markerOptions` options to make it easier to discern which line goes with which data series.

In the next chapter, we will look at pulling data from remote sources. We will also create area charts and scatterplots. Along with all of this, we will look at how trend lines work and how to create them.

2
More Line Charts, Area Charts, and Scatter Plots

In the previous chapter, we reviewed the parts of a chart and began creating line charts. We manually created data arrays and passed them into our jqPlot objects. In this chapter, we'll learn how to import data from remote sources. We will discuss what area charts, stacked area charts, and scatter plots are. Then we will learn how to implement these newly learned charts. We will also learn about trend lines. The following list details the topics covered in this chapter:

- Learn how to work with remote data sources
- Fill the area between two lines to denote expenses
- Learn about area charts and stacked area charts and how they differ
- Create an area chart showing profits by division
- Create a stacked area chart showing revenue by division
- Learn what trend lines are and how to implement them
- Discuss how scatterplot charts are different from line charts
- Create a scatterplot looking for a correlation between shares on Twitter and e-commerce conversions

Working with remote data sources

We return from lunch and decide to start on our line chart showing social media conversions. With this chart, we want to pull the data in from other sources. You start to look for some internal data sources, coming across one that returns the data as an object. We can see an excerpt of data returned by the data source. We will need to parse the object and create data arrays for jqPlot:

```
{ "twitter":[ ["2012-11-01",289],...["2012-11-30",225] ],
  "facebook":[ ["2012-11-01",27],...["2012-11-30",48] ] }
```

1. We solve this issue using a data renderer to pull our data and then format it properly for jqPlot. We can pass a function as a variable to jqPlot and when it is time to render the data, it will call this new function. We start by creating the function to receive our data and then format it. We name it `remoteDataSource`. jqPlot will pass the following three parameters to our function:

    ◦   `url`: This is the URL of our data source.

    ◦   `plot`: The jqPlot object we create is passed by reference, which means we could modify the object from within `remoteDataSource`. However, it is best to treat it as a read-only object.

    ◦   `options`: We can pass any type of option in the `dataRendererOptions` option when we create our jqPlot object. For now, we will not be passing in any options:

        ```
        <script src="../js/jqplot.dateAxisRenderer.min.js"></script>
        <script>
        $(document).ready(function(){
           var remoteDataSource = function(url, plot, options)    {
        ```

2. Next we create a new array to hold our formatted data. Then, we use the `$.ajax` method in jQuery to pull in our data. We set the `async` option to `false`. If we don't, the function will continue to run before getting the data and we'll have an empty chart:

    ```
    var data = new Array;
    $.ajax({
       async: false,
    ```

3. We set the `url` option to the `url` variable that jqPlot passed in. We also set the data type to `json`:

    ```
    url: url,
    dataType:"json",
    success: function(remoteData) {
    ```

4. Then we will take the `twitter` object in our JSON and make that the first element of our data array and make `facebook` the second element. We then return the whole array back to jqPlot to finish rendering our chart:

```
        data.push(remoteData.twitter);
        data.push(remoteData.facebook);
    }
  });
  return data;
};
```

5. With our previous charts, after the `id` attribute, we would have passed in a data array. This time, instead of passing in a data array, we pass in a URL. Then, within the options, we declare the `dataRenderer` option and set `remoteDataSource` as the value. Now when our chart is created, it will call our renderer and pass in all the three parameters we discussed earlier:

```
  var socialPlot = $.jqplot ('socialMedia', "./data/social_shares.
json",
    {
      title:'Social Media Shares',
      dataRenderer: remoteDataSource,
```

6. We create labels for both our data series and enable the legend:

```
      series:[
        { label: 'Twitter' },
        { label: 'Facebook' }
      ],
      legend: {
        show: true,
        placement: 'outsideGrid'
      },
```

7. We enable `DateAxisRenderer` for the *x* axis and set `min` to `0` on the *y* axis, so jqPlot will not extend the axis below zero:

```
      axes:{
        xaxis:{
          renderer:$.jqplot.DateAxisRenderer,
          label: 'Days in November'
        },
        yaxis: {
          min:0,
          label: 'Number of Shares'
        }
      }
    });
  });
</script>
<div id="socialMedia" style="width:600px;"></div>
```

If you are running the code samples from your filesystem in Chrome, you will get an error message similar to this:

No 'Access-Control-Allow-Origin' header is present on the requested resource.

The security settings do not allow AJAX requests to be run against files on the filesystem. It is better to use a local web server such as MAMP, WAMP, or XAMPP. This way, we avoid the access control issues. Further information about cross-site HTTP requests can be found at the Mozilla Developer Network at `https://developer.mozilla.org/en-US/docs/Web/HTTP/Access_control_CORS`.

We load this new chart in our browser and can see the result in the following screenshot:

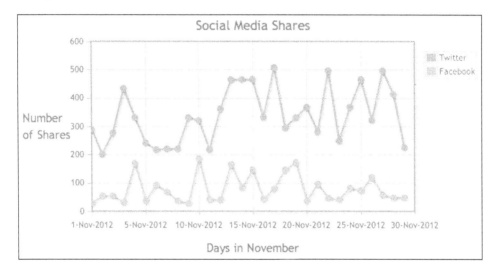

We are likely to run into cross-domain issues when trying to access remote sources that do not allow cross-domain requests. The common practice to overcome this hurdle would be to use the JSONP data type in our AJAX call. jQuery will only run JSONP calls asynchronously. This keeps your web page from hanging if a remote source stops responding. However, because jqPlot requires all the data from the remote source before continuing, we can't use cross-domain sources with our data renderers.

We start to think of ways we can use external APIs to pull in data from all kinds of sources. We make a note to contact the server guys to write some scripts to pull from the external APIs we want and pass along the data to our charts. By doing it in this way, we won't have to implement OAuth (OAuth is a standard framework used for authentication), `http://oauth.net/2`, in our web app or worry about which sources allow cross-domain access.

Adding to the project's scope

As we continue thinking up new ways to work with this data, Calvin stops by. "Hey guys, I've shown your work to a few of the regional vice-presidents and they love it." Your reply is that all of this is simply an experiment and was not designed for public consumption.

Calvin holds up his hands as if to hold our concerns at bay. "Don't worry, they know it's all in beta. They did have a couple of ideas. Can you insert in the expenses with the revenue and profit reports? They also want to see those same charts but formatted differently."

He continues, "One VP mentioned that maybe we could have one of those charts where everything under the line is filled in. Oh, and they would like to see these by Wednesday ahead of the meeting." With that, Calvin turns around and makes his customary abrupt exit.

Adding a fill between two lines

We talk through Calvin's comments. Adding in expenses won't be too much of an issue. We could simply add the expense line to one of our existing reports but that will likely not be what they want. Visually, the gap on our chart between profit and revenue should be the total amount of expenses. You mention that we could fill in the gap between the two lines. We decide to give this a try:

1. We leave the plugins and the data arrays alone. We pass an empty array into our data array as a placeholder for our expenses. Next, we update our title. After this, we add a new series object and label it `Expenses`:

```
...
    var rev_profit = $.jqplot ('revPrfChart', [revenue, profit,
[]],
    {
       title:'Monthly Revenue & Profit with Highlighted Expenses',
       series:[ { label: 'Revenue' }, { label: 'Profit' }, { label:
'Expenses' } ],
       legend: { show: true, placement: 'outsideGrid' },
```

2. To fill in the gap between the two lines, we use the `fillBetween` option. The only two required options are `series1` and `series2`. These require the positions of the two data series in the data array. So in our chart, `series1` would be `0` and `series2` would be `1`.

   The other three optional settings are: `baseSeries`, `color`, and `fill`. The `baseSeries` option tells jqPlot to place the fill on a layer beneath the given series. It will default to `0`. If you pick a series above zero, then the fill will hide any series below the fill layer:

   ```
   fillBetween: {
       series1: 0,
       series2: 1,
   ```

3. We want to assign a different value to `color` because it will default to the color of the first data series option. The color option will accept either a hexadecimal value or the `rgba` option, which allows us to change the opacity of the fill. Even though the `fill` option defaults to `true`, we explicitly set it. This option also gives us the ability to turn off the fill after the chart is rendered:

   ```
   color: "rgba(232, 44, 12, 0.5)",
   fill: true
   },
   ```

4. The settings for the rest of the chart remain unchanged:

   ```
   axes:{
       xaxis:{
           renderer:$.jqplot.DateAxisRenderer,
           label: 'Months'
       },
       yaxis:{
           label: 'Totals Dollars',
           tickOptions: {
               formatString: "$%'d"
           }
       }
   }
   });
   });
   </script>
   <div id="revPrfChart" style="width:600px;"></div>
   ```

We switch back to our web browser and load the new page. We see the result of our efforts in the following screenshot. This chart layout works but we think Calvin and the others will want something else. We decide we need to make an area chart:

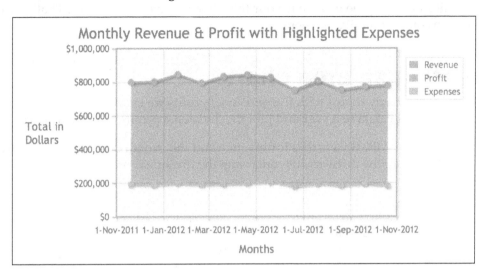

Understanding area and stacked area charts

Area charts come in two varieties. The default type of area chart is simply a modification of a line chart. Everything from the data point on the y axis all the way to zero is shaded. In the event your numbers are negative, then the data above the line up to zero is shaded in. Each data series you have is laid upon the others. Area charts are best to use when we want to compare similar elements, for example, sales by each division in our company or revenue among product categories.

The other variation of an area chart is the stacked area chart. The chart starts off being built in the same way as a normal area chart. The first line is plotted and shaded below the line to zero. The difference occurs with the remaining lines. We simply stack them. To understand what happens, consider this analogy.

Each shaded line represents a wall built to the height given in the data series. Instead of building one wall behind another, we stack them on top of each other. What can be hard to understand is the y axis. It now denotes a cumulative total, not the individual data points.

For example, if the first y value of a line is 4 and the first y value on the second line is 5, then the second point will be plotted at 9 on our y axis. Consider this more complicated example: if the y value in our first line is 2, 7 for our second line, and 4 for the third line, then the y value for our third line will be plotted at 13. That's why we need to compare similar elements.

Creating an area chart

We grab the quarterly report with the divisional profits we created this morning. We will extend the data to a year and plot the divisional profits as an area chart:

1. We remove the data arrays for revenue and the overall profit array. We also add data to the three arrays containing the divisional profits:

    ```
    <script src="../js/jqplot.dateAxisRenderer.min.js"></script>
    <script>
    $(document).ready(function(){
        var electronics = [["2011-11-20", 123487.87], ...];
        var media = [["2011-11-20", 66449.15], ...];
        var nerd_corral = [["2011-11-20", 2112.55], ...];

        var div_profit = $.jqplot ('division_profit', [media, nerd_
    corral, electronics],
        {
            title:'12 Month Divisional Profits',
    ```

2. Under `seriesDefaults`, we assign true to `fill` and `fillToZero`. Without setting `fillToZero` to `true`, the fill would continue to the bottom of the chart. With the option set, the fill will extend downward to zero on the y axis for positive values and stop. For negative data points, the fill will extend upward to zero:

    ```
        seriesDefaults: { fill: true, fillToZero: true },
        series:[ { label: 'Media & Software' }, { label: 'Nerd
    Corral' }, { label: 'Electronics' } ],
        legend: { show: true, placement: 'outsideGrid' },
    ```

3. For our x axis, we set `numberTicks` to 6. The rest of our options we leave unchanged:

    ```
        axes:{
          xaxis:{
            label: 'Months',
            renderer:$.jqplot.DateAxisRenderer,
            numberTicks: 6,
            tickOptions: { formatString: "%B" }
    ```

```
        },
        yaxis: {
            label: 'Total Dollars',
            tickOptions: { formatString: "$%'d" }
        }
    }
  });
});
</script>
<div id="division_profit" style="width:600px;"></div>
```

We review the results of our changes in our browser. These can be seen in the following screenshot:

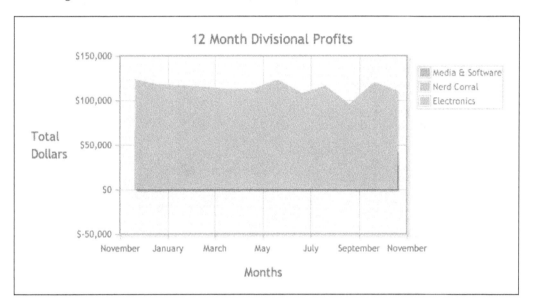

We notice something is wrong: only the **Electronics** series, shown in brown, is showing. This goes back to how area charts are built. Revisiting our wall analogy, we have built a taller wall in front of our other two walls. We need to order our data series from largest to smallest:

1. We move the **Electronics** series to be the first one in our data array:

   ```
   var div_profit = $.jqplot ('division_profit', [electronics, media,
   nerd_corral],
   ```

2. It's also hard to see where some of the lines go when they move underneath another layer. Thankfully, jqPlot has a `fillAlpha` option. We pass in a percentage in the form of a decimal and jqPlot will change the opacity of our fill area:

```
...
seriesDefaults: {
  fill: true,
  fillToZero: true,
  fillAlpha: .6
},
...
```

We reload our chart in our web browser and can see the updated changes in the following screenshot:

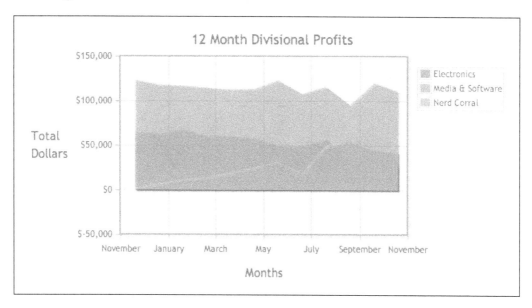

Creating a stacked area chart with revenue

Calvin stops by while we're taking a break. "Hey guys, I had a VP call and they want to see revenue broken down by division. Can we do that?" We tell him we can. "Great" he says, before turning away and leaving. We discuss this new request and realize this would be a great chance to use a stacked area chart.

We dig around and find the divisional revenue numbers Calvin wanted. We can reuse the chart we just created and just change out the data and some options.

1. We use the same variable names for our divisional data and plug in revenue numbers instead of profit. We use a new variable name for our chart object and a new `id` attribute for our div. We update our title and add the `stackSeries` option and set it to `true`:

```
var div_revenue = $.jqplot ('division_revenue', [electronics,
media, nerd_corral],
  {
    title:'12 Month Divisional Revenue',
    stackSeries: true,
```

2. We leave our series' options alone and the only option we change on our *x* axis is set `numberTicks` back to `3`:

```
    seriesDefaults: { fill: true, fillToZero: true },
    series:[ { label: 'Electronics' }, { label: 'Media & Software'
}, { label: 'Nerd Corral' } ],
    legend: { show: true, placement: 'outsideGrid' },
    axes:{
      xaxis:{
        label: 'Months',
        renderer:$.jqplot.DateAxisRenderer,
        numberTicks: 3,
        tickOptions: { formatString: "%B" }
      },
```

3. We finish our changes by updating the ID of our div container:

```
      yaxis: {
        label: 'Total Dollars',
        tickOptions: { formatString: "$%'d" }
      }
    }
  });
});
</script>
<div id="division_revenue" style="width:600px;"></div>
```

With our changes complete, we load this new chart in our browser. As we can see in the following screenshot, we have a chart with each of the data series stacked on top of each other. Because of the nature of a stacked chart, the individual data points are no longer decipherable; however, with the visualization, this is less of an issue.

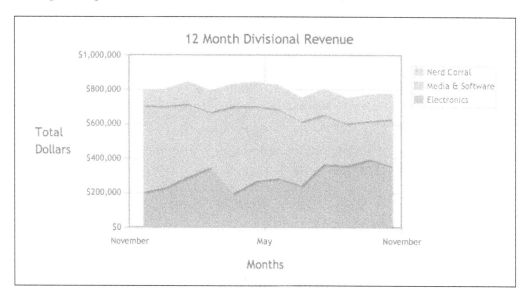

We decide that this is a good place to stop for the day. We'll start on scatterplots and trend lines tomorrow morning. As we begin gathering our things, Calvin stops by on his way out and we show him our recent work. "This is amazing. You guys are making great progress." We tell him we're going to move on to trend lines tomorrow.

"Oh, good," Calvin says. "I've had requests to show trending data for our revenue and profit. Someone else mentioned they would love to see trending data of shares on Twitter for our daily deals site. But, like you said, that can wait till tomorrow. Come on, I'll walk with you two."

Understanding trend lines

The next morning with coffee mugs in hand, we set about adding trend lines to some of our existing charts. We decide that we will take our chart with the past twelve months of revenue and profit data and add a trend line.

Trend lines are calculated by taking all the data points on the *y* axis and picking a path where the number of points on either side of the line are as close to equal as possible. By doing this, jqPlot creates a line that will generally move upward or downward moving from left to right. This allows us to see if our data is moving upwards or downwards over time. Hence, we can see if our data is "trending" up or down.

Adding trend lines

We decide to use the profit and revenue chart with two *y* axes we created yesterday:

1. We begin our updates by including the trend line plugin. We leave the data arrays as they are:

```
<script src="../js/jqplot.dateAxisRenderer.min.js"></script>
<script src="../js/jqplot.trendline.min.js"></script>
<script>
$(document).ready(function(){

  var revenue = [['2011-11-20', 800538], ['2011-12-20', 804879],
['2012-01-20', 847732], ['2012-02-20', 795758], ['2012-03-20',
835554], ['2012-04-20', 844379], ['2012-05-20', 828510], ['2012-
06-20', 753984], ['2012-07-20', 807403], ['2012-08-20', 755840],
['2012-09-20', 775304], ['2012-10-20', 781322]];

  var profit = [['2011-11-20', 192049.56], ['2011-12-20',
188744.75], ['2012-01-20', 197352.54], ['2012-02-20', 190106.74],
['2012-03-20', 193453.07], ['2012-04-20', 197249.69], ['2012-
05-20', 205480.18], ['2012-06-20', 177648.78], ['2012-07-20',
193793.82], ['2012-08-20', 183221.56], ['2012-09-20', 192797.31],
['2012-10-20', 182451.68]];
```

2. We can set the `trendline` option in `seriesDefaults` or individually within the `series` object. If we set the trend line option in `seriesDefaults`, jqPlot would generate a trend line for each data series. We just want a trend line for our revenue line, so we add the `trendline` option to our revenue series:

```
series:[
  {
    label: 'Revenue',
    trendline: {
```

3. By default, the `show` option for trend lines is set to `false`, which means we have to explicitly set it to `true`. There are quite a few options for trend lines but we'll focus on a couple we're most likely to use. We assign `#666` to `color` because the color of our trend line will default to the color of the series line. We add a label so we know which data series it is connected with. We also want the width of our line to be a bit more substantial so we set `lineWidth` to 4:

```
        show: true,
        color: '#666',
        label: 'Trend of Revenue',
        lineWidth: 4,
      }
    },
    { label: 'Profit', yaxis: 'y2axis' }
  ],
```

4. The only change to our *x* axis is with the value of `numberTicks` to 4:

```
legend: { show: true, placement: 'outsideGrid' },
axes:{
  xaxis:{
    renderer:$.jqplot.DateAxisRenderer,
    label: 'Months',
    numberTicks: 4
  },
```

5. The rest of the chart remains the same:

```
  yaxis:{
    label: 'Totals Dollars',
    tickOptions: {
      formatString: "$%'d"
    }
  },
  y2axis:{
    label: 'Totals Dollars',
    tickOptions: {
      formatString: "$%'d"
    }
  }
 }
});
});
</script>
<div id="revenueProfitChart" style="width:750px;"></div>
```

When we load the page in our browser, we see the following chart:

Initially, it would appear that revenue over the past year has been decreasing. With so few data points, it would be unwise to draw any conclusions based on our trend line.

Increasing the number of data points

We dig up revenue data that goes back to 2010. This provides us with more data points and a more accurate picture of revenue. We can reuse the chart we just created and remove the profit data series so we only have revenue on the chart.

1. We start by removing the profit data array:

```
<script src="../js/jqplot.dateAxisRenderer.min.js"></script>
<script src="../js/jqplot.trendline.min.js"></script>
<script>
$(document).ready(function(){

  var revenue = [['2010-11-20', 580538], ['2010-12-20', 604879],
  ['2011-01-20', 647732], ['2011-02-20', 695758], ['2011-03-20',
  735554], ['2011-04-20', 744379], ['2011-05-20', 728510], ['2011-
  06-20', 653984], ['2011-07-20', 707403], ['2011-08-20', 655840],
  ['2011-09-20', 675304], ['2011-10-20', 681322],['2011-11-20',
  800538], ['2011-12-20', 804879], ['2012-01-20', 847732], ['2012-
  02-20', 795758], ['2012-03-20', 835554], ['2012-04-20', 844379],
  ['2012-05-20', 828510], ['2012-06-20', 753984], ['2012-07-20',
  807403], ['2012-08-20', 755840], ['2012-09-20', 775304], ['2012-
  10-20', 781322]];
```

2. We change the object variable and the id attribute. We also remove the profit data array from the parameters:

```
var rev_chart = $.jqplot ('revenueChart', [revenue],
{
```

3. We update the title and remove the series object for the profit line:

```
title:'Monthly Revenue',
series:[
  {
    label: 'Revenue',
    trendline: {
      show: true,
      color: '#666666',
      lineWidth: 4,
    }
  }
],
```

4. With more data, our *x* axis has become crowded, so we set `numberTicks` to 6:

```
axes:{
  xaxis:{
    renderer:$.jqplot.DateAxisRenderer,
    label: 'Months',
    numberTicks: 6
  },
  yaxis:{
    label: 'Totals Dollars',
    tickOptions: { formatString: "$%'d" }
  }
}
});
});
</script>
```

5. We complete our changes by changing the ID of our div and decreasing the width:

```
<div id="revenueChart" style="width:600px;"></div>
```

After making our changes, we load the new chart in our browser. We can see the results of our work appear in the following screenshot:

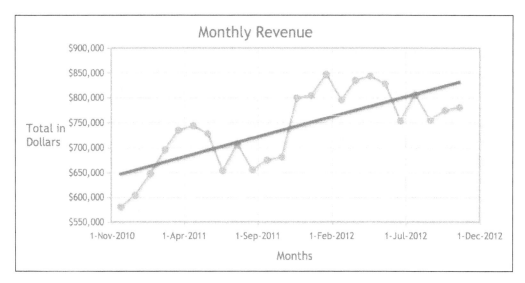

We can see that revenue has shown an upward trend over the past two years. This is a good time to remind ourselves that data can be manipulated to say almost anything we want. That's why there are so many different chart types. Some data sets may lead to incorrect conclusions based on how they are rendered. Also, charts are merely a representation of the data. There are many underlying issues that cannot be expressed in charts, with the potential to skew visualizations.

Understanding scatterplot charts

We decide to move onto scatterplots, which are also known as scatter charts. These look very similar to line charts but they represent data differently. Line charts show data in a linear fashion, meaning it starts at one point and moves to another point in a given direction. If we are charting data that happens at given time periods, our date line will not jump back and forth in time. On the other hand, scatterplots show trending data but they do it by comparing the data points.

For example, we might look at gross profit in relation to the number of retail stores, or the amount of time a customer spends in the store compared to the total dollar amount they spend. Scatterplots with trend lines allow us to take two datasets that may not appear related, plot them, and see if there is any correlation between them.

Extending the data renderer

The IT department e-mailed us while we were working on our chart. They created some data feeds for us to pull the social media conversion numbers that we need. We are going to create a scatterplot with the total number of daily shares on Twitter and the total conversions. The new data source returns an array so we won't need to change anything.

Our original `remoteDataSource` function was tailored specifically for our other social media chart. We decide to extract the functionality to retrieve remote data and also make use of `dataRendererOptions`.

To start off, we create a new file called `functions.js` inside our `js` folder. We will save our new function, `remoteDataCallback`, in this file so we can reuse the code.

We remove the code that parsed the JSON object. In its place, we assign `options.dataCallback` to our `data` array. Later, when we create our chart, we will pass a function called `dataConversion` into `dataCallback`. We pass `remoteData`, which is the JSON object, as a parameter to our `dataCallback` method:

```
var remoteDataCallback = function(url, plot, options) {
  var data = new Array;
  $.ajax({
    async: false,
    url: url,
    dataType:"json",
    success: function(remoteData) {
      data = options.dataCallback(remoteData);
    }
  });
  return data;
};
```

Creating a scatterplot chart

Now that we have created our new function file, we are ready to begin building our chart. A scatterplot chart is rendered the same in jqPlot as a normal line chart except that we turn off the lines connecting our data points.

1. We start our code by including the trend line plugin and our new `functions.js` file. We create a new data conversion function called `dataConversion`. Since `remoteDataCallback` is passing back an array, we simply need to wrap it in another array for jqPlot:

    ```
    <script src="../js/jqplot.trendline.min.js"></script>
    <script src="../js/functions.js"></script>
    <script>
    function dataConversion(remoteData) {
      var data = new Array();
      data[0] = remoteData;
      return data;
    }
    ```

2. We create our chart object and pass in the URL of the data feed that IT created for us:

```
$(document).ready(function(){
  var share_conversions = $.jqplot ('share_conversions', "./data/
share_conversions.json",
  {
    title:'Conversions from Total Shares',
```

3. We assign our new function `remoteDataCallback` to `dataRenderer`. Next we create an object called `dataCallback` and assign it `dataConversion`. This goes in the `dataRendererOptions` option. When our chart is rendered, jqPlot will call `remoteDataCallback` and then it will pass our JSON object, `remoteData`, to `dataConversion`:

```
dataRenderer: remoteDataCallback,
dataRendererOptions: { dataCallback: dataConversion },
```

4. For our series object, we set `showLine` to `false` on our data series to turn off the line. We also create an object for our trend line:

```
series:[
  {
    showLine: false,
    trendline: {
      show: true,
      color: '#666666',
      lineWidth: 4
    }
  },
],
```

5. We set labels for our axes, and since we are dealing with noncurrency numbers, we don't need to format them:

```
axes:{
  xaxis:{ label: 'Shares on Twitter' },
  yaxis:{ label: 'Conversions' }
}
});
});
</script>
<div id="share_conversions" style="width:600px;"></div>
```

We are eager to see how our chart turns out. We load the page in our browser and see the resulting scatterplot shown in the following screenshot:

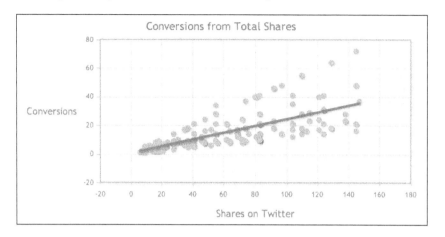

Intuition would lead us to believe that as the number of social shares on Twitter increase, the number of conversions also increase. The numbers seem to agree with this hypothesis but equally, the numbers could have just as easily shown a decrease in conversions. This is why scatterplots are ideal; we start with an idea of what we expect the data to tell us and then attempt to test it with a scatterplot and trend line.

We call Calvin to have him take a look at what we've got. He stops by about fifteen minutes later. "This is awesome guys. Can you e-mail me links to these charts? Once the VPs look at this tomorrow, we'll give you some feedback."

A smile appears on Calvin's face. "All this has put me in a really generous mood. Let's swing by the sandwich shop down the street and I'll pick up the tab." We look at each other; we're not going to turn down a free lunch.

Learning questions

1. Which three parameters does jqPlot pass to the function that we create to pull our remote data?

2. Why can't we use JSONP to access remote data sources?

3. What do we pass to the dataRenderer option?

4. What do you need to keep in mind when creating an area chart?

5. Where do we enable trend lines in our plot object?

Summary

In this chapter, we learned how to work with remote data sources. With this knowledge, we created a reusable function to retrieve data. We learned about the `fillBetween` method and then went on to discuss the different area charts and created examples of each.

We gained an understanding of what trend lines are and looked at how the results can change depending on the number of data points. Along the way, we took note of some of the interpretation issues that can arise based on how data is visualized. We concluded the chapter by discussing scatterplot charts and looked for correlations in our data with the chart we created.

In the next chapter, we will learn about bar charts and the best uses for them. We will also look at ways to expand the functionality of our charts with click and hover events.

3
Bar Charts and Digging into Data

In the previous chapters, we learned how to create line charts and area charts. In this chapter, we will turn our attention to bar charts. We'll look at different options to format our axes and ticks. After mastering bar charts, we will create event handlers for various jqPlot events. With these event handlers, we will extend the functionality of our charts. In this chapter, we will specifically learn the following topics:

- Build a basic chart based on return options for products
- Add additional data points and style our chart to work with the increasing data
- Create a bar chart showing multiple data series
- Add a trend line to our chart with multiple data series to see how they are trending
- Add an event handler to our bar chart to expand on the data selected from the chart
- Revisit our stacked area chart and add an event handler to show all the data points in a table

Building bars of data

While at lunch, Calvin took several phone calls. One near the end of lunch was from Sara, VP of Inventory. Her department is facing issues with higher than normal returns. She has a team investigating the problem, but she wants help. She wants a chart showing how much money is lost to returns and the reasons for the returns. She'd like the charts by the end of the meeting on Friday so that she can present the problem to the whole team. She needs their buy-in and help to work toward a solution.

Calvin relays this information to us as we walk back to the office. "She said she was going to e-mail a spreadsheet with the past six months' data in it. Can you do your thing and make Sara look like a rockstar? Her department is the most ignored, but it's the backbone of the company." We tell him we'll do our best.

By the time we get back to our desks, we have an e-mail waiting for us. We open the spreadsheet and see the following data:

Damaged Item	$15,876.98
Defective Item	$26,078.41
Gift	$6,397.06
Not Correct Item	$12,876.60

After looking over the data, we decide that our best choice is a bar chart. Bar charts are best used when we have categorical data to compare. We can compare various data points in one series or multiple data series. With this chart, we will be able to compare the dollar amounts in each category listed previously, so we will have just one data series. It is also possible to have multiple data series in each category, such as a different bar for each product category, and these data series grouped by regions.

1. We start by including the `categoryAxisRenderer` and `barRenderer` plugins. These extend jqPlot to allow us to group our *x* axis by categories and create a bar chart:

```
<script src="../js/jqplot.categoryAxisRenderer.min.js"></script>
<script src="../js/jqplot.barRenderer.min.js"></script>
<script>

$(document).ready(function(){
```

2. We include our array containing the data points. Since we are using `categoryAxisRenderer`, we pass a string as the *x* value instead of a number or date:

```
var returns = [['Damaged Item', 15876.98], ['Defective Item',
26078.41], ['Gift', 6397.06], ['Not Correct Item', 12876.60]];

var product_returns = $.jqplot ('product_returns', [returns],
{
    title:'Total Cost of Product Returns over 6 months',
```

3. We assign `BarRenderer` to the `renderer` option for our one data series. If we were to include multiple data series, we could include this in `seriesDefaults` so we'd only have to include it once:

```
series: [ { renderer:$.jqplot.BarRenderer } ],
```

4. Since we are using categories for the *x* axis, we need to enable
    `CategoryAxisRenderer` as the renderer for the *x* axis:

```
axes:{
  xaxis:{ renderer: $.jqplot.CategoryAxisRenderer },
  yaxis: {
    label: 'Totals Dollars',
    tickOptions: { formatString: "$%'d" }
  }
}
});
});
</script>

<div id="product_returns" style="width:600px;"></div>
```

> We can mix and match data renderers. If we had multiple data
> series, we could render a bar chart for the first series and use a
> line chart for the second.

We load the page in our browser and see the following result:

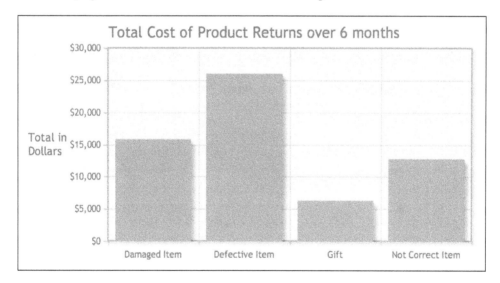

Adding styles to our bar chart

We start thinking about how we can plot revenue and profit as a bar graph, when Calvin stops by. He takes a look at what we have. "Oh, I forgot. Sara sent a follow-up e-mail. There were a couple of categories that were left out of the spreadsheet. Let me forward that to you guys."

Calvin looks for the e-mail on his phone while he keeps talking, "Also, can you create a chart showing revenue grouped by product categories? She'll send over the data later this afternoon. OK, sent. I'll check back later," he says while walking out of the office.

We receive the second e-mail and open the updated spreadsheet. There are two new categories and their totals are much higher than the others. We can see why Sara is so concerned:

Damaged Item	$15,876.98
Defective Item	$26,078.41
Gift	$6,397.06
Not Correct Item	$12,876.60
No Longer Wanted/Needed	$41,654.67
Other / No Reason Given	$72,245.63

With all these categories on the x axis, we will not be able to read them all. So, we are going to rotate the labels to make them easier to read. We will also add point labels so that the y value of each bar appears above the bar. With these changes in mind, we set about updating our chart by executing the following steps:

1. We start by adding in the `pointLabels`, `canvasTextRenderer`, and `canvasAxisTickRenderer` plugins. The canvas plugins place our ticks on a `canvas` element instead of a div element. This allows us to rotate our text:

    ```
    <script src="../js/jqplot.pointLabels.min.js"></script>
    <script src="../js/jqplot.canvasTextRenderer.min.js"></script>
    <script src="../js/jqplot.canvasAxisTickRenderer.min.js"></script>
    <script>
    ```

2. We add the two new categories and the dollar amounts to our data array:

```
$(document).ready(function(){
  var returns = [['Damaged Item', 15876.98], ['No Longer Wanted/
Needed', 41654.67], ['Defective Item', 26078.41], ['Gift',
6397.06], ['Not Correct Item', 12876.60], ['Other / No Reason
Given', 72245.63]];

  var product_returns = $.jqplot ('product_returns', [returns],
  {
    title:'Total Cost of Product Returns over 6 months',
```

3. To allow our ticks to rotate, we need to pass the CanvasAxisTickRenderer plugin to tickRenderer. Once we do this, we create tickOptions, and set the angle option to -30:

```
axesDefaults: {
  tickRenderer: $.jqplot.CanvasAxisTickRenderer ,
  tickOptions: { angle: -30 }
},
```

4. We create the pointLabels object under seriesDefaults, and set show to true:

```
seriesDefaults:{
  renderer:$.jqplot.BarRenderer,
  pointLabels: { show: true }
},
```

5. We want a little more space between each category, so we set barMargin to 20. The default is 10. By default, jqPlot adds a little bit of shadow to each data point, whether it is a point on a line or a bar. We increase shadowAlpha to 0.8, which causes the bars to look three-dimensional:

```
series: [
  {
    rendererOptions: {
      barMargin: 20,
      shadowAlpha: 0.8
    }
  }
],
```

6. Finally, we want to add some padding on our *y* axis. If we don't, the chart will autosize and not leave enough room for the point label on our bar that reaches $72,000.

There are three options to set padding: pad, padMin, and padMax. The pad option will add padding to the upper and lower bounds of the *y* axis. The padMin option will only add padding to the lower bound, and padMax will add padding to the upper bound. Since we want padding only at the top of our chart, we set padMax to 1.2:

```
axes:{
    xaxis:{ renderer: $.jqplot.CategoryAxisRenderer },
    yaxis: {
        label: 'Totals Dollars',
        padMax: 1.2,
        tickOptions: { formatString: "$%'d" }
    }
  }
});
});
</script>

<div id="product_returns" style="width:600px;"></div>
```

After all our hard work, we load the chart in our browser and see the following results. The **Other / No Reason Given** category is concerning.

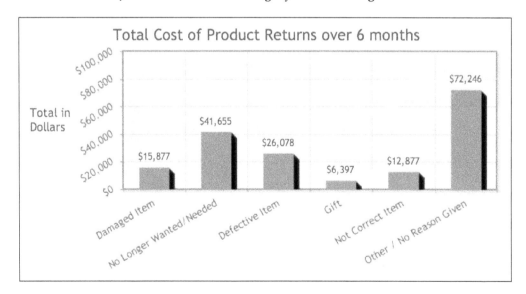

By rotating our categories on the *x* axis, our tick marks do not run together like before. By using `barMargin`, we add some space between each category. With `padMax`, we add space to the top of our chart for point labels, which makes the value for each bar more accessible. Finally, the dark shadow on our bars makes the values stand out.

Creating charts with multiple data series

As we begin thinking about how to expand this report, we get another e-mail from Sara.

"Hey, I got to thinking and we've cut purchasing in some product categories. We're taking heat from the rest of the team because they think we're being too cautious. Can you create a chart with the four product categories I included? You'll also find revenue numbers for the last six quarters."

We start thinking about how this chart will work. We know that each category will be a data series, and so, there will be four bars listed for each quarter for a total of 24 bars. With the default margins and padding, our bars will be resized to tiny slivers. So, we'll need to change some formatting. Also, since we have multiple data series, we will have to set the ticks for our *x* axis separately. With these parameters, we set about building our chart executing the following steps:

1. We include the plugins we've been using:

   ```
   <script src="../js/jqplot.categoryAxisRenderer.min.js"></script>
   <script src="../js/jqplot.barRenderer.min.js"></script>
   <script src="../js/jqplot.canvasTextRenderer.min.js"></script>
   <script src="../js/jqplot.canvasAxisTickRenderer.min.js"></script>
   ```

2. We move on to include our four data series and an array of the labels for our ticks:

   ```
   ...
   <script>
   $(document).ready(function(){
     var dvds = [546643.33, 517902.14, 482774.32, 455892.62,
   438679.00, 406907.18];
     var cds = [398583.39, 386552.99, 372738.46, 359209.91,
   336457.82, 327396.58];
     var tvs = [378583.39, 346552.99, 368164.98, 371856.60,
   366457.82, 327396.58];
     var computers = [563621.35, 540214.96, 589978.66, 637114.31,
   621279.49, 599837.31];
     var ticks = ['Q2 - 2011', 'Q3 - 2011', 'Q4 - 2011', 'Q1 - 2012',
   'Q2 - 2012', 'Q3 - 2012'];
   ```

3. We create our jqPlot object and pass in our data arrays. We also set our ticks to be rotated at -30 degrees:

```
var rev_category = $.jqplot ('rev_category', [dvds, cds, tvs,
computers],
  {
    title:'Quarterly Revenue by Product',
    axesDefaults: {
      tickRenderer: $.jqplot.CanvasAxisTickRenderer,
      tickOptions: { angle: -30 }
    },
```

4. Just as we have padding options for our axes, we also have a padding option for our bars along with the barMargin option discussed earlier. While barMargin adds space between categories, barPadding adds spacing between the bars within a category.

   We set barMargin to 6 and barPadding to 2, which will give us a little bit of space between our categories and individual bars. We also set shadow to false because our bars are so close together:

```
    seriesDefaults:{
      renderer:$.jqplot.BarRenderer,
      rendererOptions: {
        barMargin: 6,
        barPadding: 2,
        shadow: false
      }
    },
    series: [
      { label: 'DVDs/Blu-ray' },
      { label: 'Music CDs' },
      { label: 'TVs' },
      { label: 'Computers' }
    ],
```

5. For this chart, we set the legend placement to insideGrid. This will cause our plot to get bigger because it is not trying to accommodate the legend. We also make use of the location option. By setting it to nw, our legend will appear in the top-left corner of the legend. If we pick s, it will appear at the bottom of our plot in the middle:

```
    legend: {
      show: true, placement: 'insideGrid', location: 'nw'
    },
```

6. We set the `ticks` option on our *x* axis to the `ticks` array we added earlier. Finally, we don't want our legend to cover our bars, so we set `padMax` on the *y* axis to `1.6`:

```
axes:{
    xaxis:{ label: 'Quarters', renderer: $.jqplot.
CategoryAxisRenderer, ticks: ticks },
        yaxis: {
          label: 'Totals Dollars',
          padMax: 1.6,
          tickOptions: { formatString: "$%'d" }
        }
      }
   });
});
</script>

<div id="rev_category" style="width:700px;"></div>
```

After loading the new chart in our browser, we see that all our work gives us the following result:

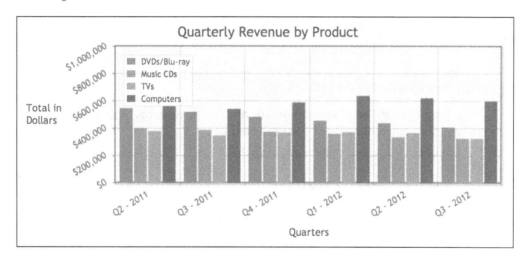

One of the benefits of bar charts is that the values they express are more discreet. Earlier, we plotted revenue data on line graphs. By connecting the data points with lines, it gives the impression that revenue moves in a straight line between each date interval. Bar charts group all the data for an interval into a bar, and they better represent data that might fluctuate greatly during the intervals shown.

Adding trend lines to selected product categories

We can tell from the chart we just created that TVs and computers sell better than DVDs and CDs. However, with so many bars and so little perceived movement in the data between quarters, this chart doesn't tell us much more. This leads us to think about how we can make the chart more interactive. We conclude that adding a trend line to one data series will help us see whether revenue is trending up or down for a given category.

We don't want to create separate charts for each product category; so we will just add a drop-down menu with each product category. When the dropdown changes, it will submit the form and reload the page. We'll add functions to determine which drop-down item is selected, and then create a trend line for the corresponding data series. We decide to start with our query string parsing function:

1. We open `functions.js` and create `getQueryStringVar` that accepts the parameter `name`. This is the name of the value from our query string that is created when we submit our form. Next, we pull in the query string and split it into the array, `hashes`:

   ```
   function getQueryStringVar(name){
     var vars = [];
     var hash = [];
     var hashes = window.location.href.slice( window.location.href.
   indexOf('?') + 1 ).split('&');
   ```

2. We loop through each key-value pair and create an array with each value. Then, we return the value of the selected key:

   ```
   for(var i = 0; i < hashes.length; i++)
   {
     hash = hashes[i].split('=');
     vars.push(hash[0]);
     vars[hash[0]] = decodeURI(hash[1]);
   }
   return vars[name];
   }
   ```

3. We switch back to the code for our chart. We include the `trendline` plugin and `functions.js` file along with our other plugins:

   ```
   <script src="../js/jqplot.categoryAxisRenderer.min.js"></script>
   <script src="../js/jqplot.barRenderer.min.js"></script>
   <script src="../js/jqplot.canvasTextRenderer.min.js"></script>
   ```

```
<script src="../js/jqplot.canvasAxisTickRenderer.min.js"></script>
<script src="../js/jqplot.trendline.min.js"></script>
<script src="../js/functions.js"></script>
```

4. Next, we include the arrays for each product category:

```
<script>
$(document).ready(function(){
  var dvds = [546643.33, 517902.14, 482774.32, 455892.62,
438679.00, 406907.18];
  var cds = [398583.39, 386552.99, 372738.46, 359209.91,
336457.82, 327396.58];
  var tvs = [378583.39, 346552.99, 368164.98, 371856.60,
366457.82, 327396.58];
  var computers = [563621.35, 540214.96, 589978.66, 637114.31,
621279.49, 599837.31];
```

5. After that, we create the array `trendline` to contain an object for each of our product category data series. Next, we declare the variable `selectedIndex`, which uses our new `getQueryStringVar` function to get the existing value of our query string parameter, `trendline`. If `trendline` is not set, we set `selectedIndex` to 0:

```
  var trendline = new Array();
  var selectedIndex = getQueryStringVar('trendline') || 0;
```

6. Next, we create a loop to step through each option in the dropdown. When we begin each step, we create an object in the current element of our `trendline` array. We create default values for our `show` and `label` parameters in the new object. These parameters match the options available to us under the trend line option in jqPlot:

```
$("#trendline option").each(function(i, option) {
  trendline[i] = new Object();
  trendline[i].show = false;
  trendline[i].label = '';
```

7. After we create our object, we check whether the current element is the selected index. If it is, we select the option in the drop-down. Then for the current `trendline` object, we set `show` to `true`, pull the text from the drop-down option, and set this option to our label:

```
  if(i == selectedIndex) {
    $('#trendline > option:eq('+i+')').prop('selected', true);
    trendline[i].show = true;
    trendline[i].label = 'Trend: ' + $('#trendline >
option:eq('+i+')').text();
  }
});
```

8. We create an array for our tick labels and set the defaults for the axes:

```
var ticks = ['Q2 - 2011', 'Q3 - 2011', 'Q4 - 2011', 'Q1 - 2012',
'Q2 - 2012', 'Q3 - 2012'];

var rev_category = $.jqplot ('rev_category', [dvds, cds, tvs,
computers],
{
  title:'Quarterly Revenue by Product Category',
  axesDefaults: {
    tickRenderer: $.jqplot.CanvasAxisTickRenderer,
    tickOptions: { angle: -30 }
  },
```

9. We set the `trendline` option in `seriesDefaults` so that trend lines will be available on any given series with the set color and line width:

```
seriesDefaults:{
    renderer:$.jqplot.BarRenderer,
    rendererOptions: {
      barMargin: 6,
      barPadding: 2,
      shadow: false
    },
    trendline: {
      color: '#111',
      lineWidth: 4,
    }
  },
```

10. Then, in each series, we set the `show` option to match the corresponding parameter in our `trendline` array, and do the same for the label:

```
series: [
    { label: 'DVDs/Blu-ray', trendline: {
        show: trendline[0].show, label: trendline[0].label
      }
    },
    { label: 'Music CDs' , trendline: {
        show: trendline[1].show, label: trendline[1].label
      }
    },
    { label: 'TVs' , trendline: {
        show: trendline[2].show, label: trendline[2].label
      }
    },
    { label: 'Computers' , trendline: {
```

```
            show: trendline[3].show, label: trendline[3].label
        }
    }
],
```

11. For this chart, we place the legend in the lower-left corner and set `padMax` for our *y* axis so that the legend will not cover the top of our bars:

```
    legend: { show: true, placement: 'insideGrid', location: 'sw'
},
    axes:{
        xaxis:{ label: 'Quarters', renderer: $.jqplot.
CategoryAxisRenderer, ticks: ticks },
        yaxis: {
            label: 'Totals Dollars',
            padMax: 1,
            tickOptions: { formatString: "$%'d" }
        }
    }
});
```

12. With our chart complete, we create an event handler so that when our drop-down menu is changed, it will submit the form:

```
    $("#trendline").change(function() {
        $("#form").submit();
    });

});
</script>
```

13. We finish the HTML by creating the dropdown to change trend lines and wrap it all in a form. The value of each option matches the position of the data series array for our chart:

```
<form action="1168_03_04.html" method="GET" id="form">
    <select id="trendline" name="trendline">
        <option value='0'>DVDs/Blu-ray</option>
        <option value='1'>Music CDs</option>
        <option value='2'>TVs</option>
        <option value='3'>Computers</option>
    </select>
</form>

<div id="rev_category" style="width:700px;"></div>
```

We test our chart, and a trend line for **DVDs/Blu-ray** is rendered since we did not pass a query string. Viewing the following results, we see that revenue shows a downward trend for **DVDs/Blu-ray**:

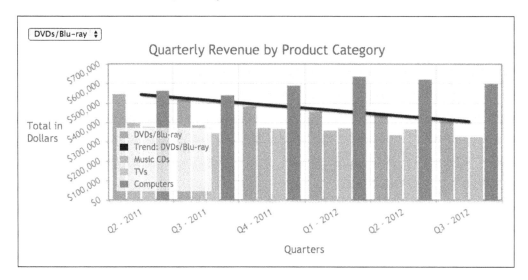

We try another data series and select **Computers** to render a new trend line. From the following screenshot, we can see that revenue shows an upward trend for **Computers**:

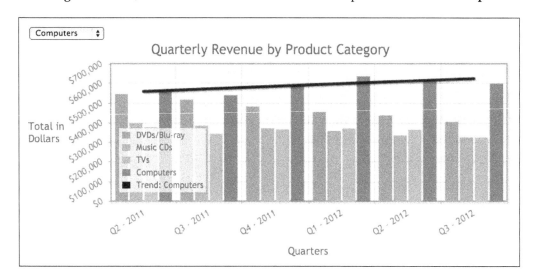

It's close to quitting time, so we decide that now will be a good time to wrap up. Calvin stops by to review our work. As we walk out with him, he comments, "What you have done is amazing. Sara and the others will be ecstatic. They are going to love what you've done. Just be ready for more work. Now that they know what you are capable of, they are going to send a lot more your way."

Expanding our datasets with event handlers

We come to work on Wednesday and spend the morning catching up on work that we put off while we worked on these charts. The VPs are scheduled to meet this afternoon.

The morning is busy and we work through our normal lunch break. We finally get away at about 2 o'clock. We walk back into our office around 3 and find Calvin waiting for us. "Good news first. They loved what you've done, Sara especially. The bar graph showing the losses really got the other VP's attention. This leads to the bad news. Well, it's not actually bad news. It's more like the next step. Can you pull up that chart?"

We sit down at the computer and pull up the chart. Calvin continues while pointing at the screen, "So, like I said, Sara loved this. What she wants to know is if there is any way we can drill down into the various bars? She's envisioning clicking on a bar and it breaks out the loss numbers by region. Her team is seeing evidence that a large percentage of returns occur in a few select regions. The team is suspicious, and Sara wants to represent this in a chart."

We tell Calvin we can and we'll work on that this afternoon. "Also," Calvin continues, "they loved the stacked chart with the revenue by division. Is there any way you can show the numbers for each month when you hover over the area?" We tell him we can do this as well. "Great. Well, I'll leave you to it." With that, he walks out of the office.

As I sit down, you mention that we received an e-mail from Sara. She sent over the regional breakdowns for each return reason. We will add a second chart under our first chart. When a user clicks on a bar, the page will reload and send the selected index as a value in our query string.

1. We open the code for our existing chart and include `functions.js` because we need our query string parsing function:

   ```
   <script src="../js/functions.js"></script>
   ...
   ```

2. After the code to build our first chart, we create an event handler for `jqplotDataClick` using the jQuery on method. jqPlot passes the four parameters of `ev`, `seriesIndex`, `pointIndex`, and `data` to the callback method inside the event handler:

```
var product_returns = $.jqplot ('product_returns', [returns], {
    ...
}
$('#product_returns').on('jqplotDataClick',
    function (ev, seriesIndex, pointIndex, data) {
```

   - ° The `ev` object contains all the object variables for the event triggering the callback.

   - ° The second parameter, `seriesIndex`, is an integer denoting the data series we click in the chart's data array. Since this chart only has one data series, `seriesIndex` will return 0 no matter which bar we click on.

   - ° The third parameter is `pointIndex`. This returns the index of the bar that was clicked on.

   - ° Finally, we have `data`. This is an array of the *x* and *y* axes values for the bar that was clicked on.

3. Inside our callback method, we use `window.location` to reload our page. We append `pointIndex` as a query string value:

```
        window.location = "1168_03_05.html?reason="+pointIndex;
    }
);
```

4. Next, we include the formatted data series for our second chart separated out by regions. Each element in the array matches with a return reason and dollar amount in the first data array:

```
    var region_breakdown = new Array();

    region_breakdown[0] = [['Southwest', 3175.40], ['California',
6350.79], ['Northwest', 3969.25], ['West Central', 2381.55]];
    region_breakdown[1] = [['Southwest', 8330.93], ['California',
27075.54], ['Northwest', 4165.47], ['West Central', 2082.73]];
    region_breakdown[2] = [['Southwest', 5215.68], ['California',
10431.36], ['Northwest', 6519.60], ['West Central', 3911.76]];
    region_breakdown[3] = [['Southwest', 1279.41], ['California',
2558.82], ['Northwest', 1599.27], ['West Central', 959.56]];
```

```
   region_breakdown[4] = [['Southwest', 2575.32], ['California',
5150.64], ['Northwest', 3219.15], ['West Central', 1931.49]];
   region_breakdown[5] = [['Southwest', 7224.56], ['California',
43347.38], ['Northwest', 18061.41], ['West Central', 3612.28]];
```

5. Like our other chart, we call `getQueryStringVar`. If no value is passed in, we want it to be `false`. We create an `if` statement so that the second chart is not rendered when the page first loads:

```
var selectedIndex = getQueryStringVar('reason') || false;


if(selectedIndex) {
```

6. The options for this chart are almost identical to the first chart, but for the current one we pass in the corresponding regional data series. We also access the return reason label from the first chart. This way the user will know what return reason was clicked on:

```
var region_returns = $.jqplot ('region_returns', [region_
breakdown[selectedIndex]],
    {
    title:'Product Returns by Region over 6 months<br>Reason:
'+returns[selectedIndex][0],
        axesDefaults: {
          tickRenderer: $.jqplot.CanvasAxisTickRenderer,
          tickOptions: { angle: -30 }
        },
        seriesDefaults:{ renderer:$.jqplot.BarRenderer },
        series: [
          {
            renderer:$.jqplot.BarRenderer,
            rendererOptions: { shadowAlpha: 0.8 }
          }
        ],
```

7. Next, we format the *y* axis to display dollar values and add a label to the *y* axis. We conclude by adding a new div to hold our regional chart:

```
        axes:{
          xaxis:{ renderer: $.jqplot.CategoryAxisRenderer },
          yaxis: {
            label: 'Totals Dollars',
            tickOptions: { formatString: "$%'d" }
          }
        }
```

```
        });
    }

});
</script>

<div id="product_returns" style="width:600px;"></div>
<div id="region_returns" style="width:500px;"></div>
```

We load the page and click on the **Defective Item** bar. The page reloads and we see the charts shown in the following screenshot. The numbers for California are high but do not seem too out of the ordinary.

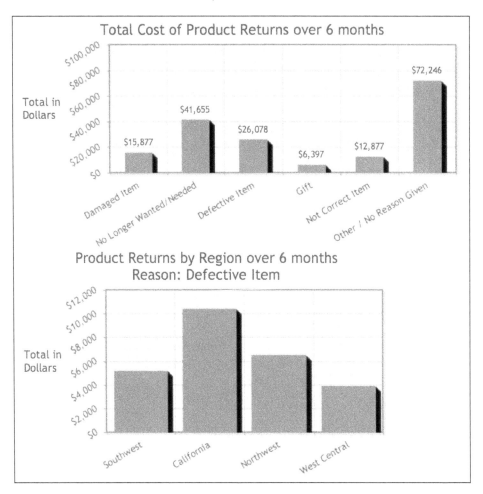

Next, we click on the **Other / No Reason Given** bar since it has the highest numbers. After the page loads, we see the results shown in the following screenshot. This chart tells a very interesting story, with over half of the returns of this region occurring in California.

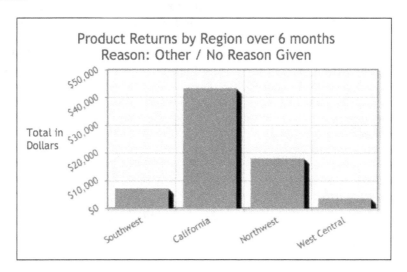

We know that the first question out of the mouths of the VPs will be, "Why are these numbers so high?" We'll have to answer candidly, "We don't know." Some people may slip into the belief that charts are supposed to explain why things are happening. The real goal of data visualization is to represent what is happening. By attempting to make the data easier to understand, we help those analyzing the data to develop a hypothesis to explain the data.

Adding an event handler for our stacked area chart

We wrap up the chart and move on to working on the stacked area chart from yesterday. We will create an event handler for the `jqplotDataHighlight` method. When a user hovers over a stacked area, we will populate a table with the current series data.

There are a few differences between this event handler and the one we used with our bar chart. We will use `seriesIndex` instead of `pointIndex` to access the data we need. For stacked charts, nothing is passed through `pointIndex`, so it will return `null`. Also, with the `data` parameter, it is an array of all the data points for the highlighted line.

Since we passed in date values originally, we might expect to have access to them in our callback. Not quite; when jqPlot takes in the data, it converts all of the date values to Unix timestamps. So, what we get in our callback are these timestamps.

We start by opening the file with our stacked chart. Below the existing chart, we set about adding in our new code, as explained in the following steps:

1. In our table, we want to include the series label in the table caption. Then, we want the month, year, and the dollar amount in each row. First, we create an array with all the months of the year:

```
var monthNames = [ "January", "February", "March", "April",
"May", "June", "July", "August", "September", "October",
"November", "December" ];
```

2. Next, we start our callback method by resetting the table caption and table rows:

```
$('#division_revenue').on('jqplotDataHighlight',
    function (ev, seriesIndex, pointIndex, data) {
      $('#divisional_data caption').html('');
      $('#divisional_data tbody tr').remove();
```

3. We then move on to create a loop that steps through each element in the highlighted data array. Then, we create a `Date` object from our timestamp:

```
$.each(data, function(i, datum) {
    var date = new Date(datum[0]);
```

4. After that, we use the `getMonth` method and pass it as the index for our `monthNames` array. Once we have the name, we concatenate the year and the dollar amount and append that to the table body:

```
var row = '<tr><td>';
row += monthNames[date.getMonth()];
row += ', '+date.getFullYear()+'</td>';
row += '<td class="right">$'+datum[1].toFixed(2);
row += '</td></tr>';
$('#divisional_data tbody').append(row);
});
```

5. Once we finish with our loop, we retrieve the label of the highlighted series. We access it through our plot object, `div_revenue`. To get to the correct series in our object, we pass in `seriesIndex`. We finish by unhiding our table:

```
$('#divisional_data caption')
    .html(div_revenue.series[seriesIndex].label);
$('#divisional_data').show();
  }
);
```

6. After our highlight method, we create a callback method for the `jqplotDataUnhighlight` event. When a user hovers away from a series, we want to clear out the table and hide it:

```
$('#division_revenue').on('jqplotDataUnhighlight',
    function (ev) {
        $('#divisional_data caption').html('');
        $('#divisional_data tbody tr').remove();
        $('#divisional_data').hide();
    }
);
```

7. When the page first loads, we want our table hidden, so we call the `hide` method on our table:

```
$('#divisional_data').hide();
});
</script>
```

8. We finish by creating our table and some styles to make our table appear next to our chart. Once we are done with our prototypes, we pull out our inline and embedded CSS styles into a separate file:

```
<div id="division_revenue" style="float:left;width:600px;
display:inline-block"></div>
<table id="divisional_data" class="div_data" style="">
<caption></caption>
<thead>
  <tr>
    <th>Month</th>
    <th>Dollar Amount</th>
  </tr>
</thead>
  <tbody></tbody>
</table>

<style>
    table.div_data {
        min-width:300px;
        float:left;
    }
    td.div_data, th.div_data {
        padding:0px 5px;
    }
    td.right {
        text-align: right;
    }
</style>
```

We reload the page, and when we hover over the **Electronics** area, the table is populated with the correct data:

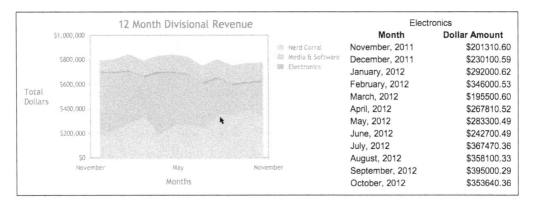

12 Month Divisional Revenue		Electronics	
		Month	**Dollar Amount**
		November, 2011	$201310.60
		December, 2011	$230100.59
		January, 2012	$292000.62
		February, 2012	$346000.53
		March, 2012	$195500.60
		April, 2012	$267810.52
		May, 2012	$283300.49
		June, 2012	$242700.49
		July, 2012	$367470.36
		August, 2012	$358100.33
		September, 2012	$395000.29
		October, 2012	$353640.36

Thinking about all the data Sara sent us, we can visualize it in several different ways. With our new roles as data analysts, we decide to do further research on data visualization. We find a couple of books by Stephen Few. He writes on simple techniques to visualize data in an understandable way. One of his books, *Now You See It: Simple Visualization Techniques for Quantitative Analysis*, which can be found at http://www.amazon.com/gp/product/0970601980, is very beneficial.

We have done all we can for the day. We will look at horizontal bar charts and stacked bar charts tomorrow. These will provide us with additional options to represent Sara's data.

Learning questions

1. How do you enable labels for your data points?

2. What renderer is necessary in order to rotate your tick labels?

3. What render option will you set to make the bars in your bar chart appear three-dimensional?

4. How did we show the user that revenue was increasing or decreasing?

5. For which two events in jqPlot did we create event handlers?

6. How else can you represent the product return reasons and the regional data in a bar chart?

7. Think back to our chart showing reasons for product returns. If you had all the data available, what might be some other criteria you would look at to determine why the returns were so high?

Summary

In this chapter, we discussed when to use bar charts. We built a basic chart based on return options for products. After adding more data points to our returns chart, we learned how to rotate the ticks of our axes. We also learned how to add spaces around our categories as well as between each individual bar using `barMargin` and `barPadding`.

We created a bar chart showing multiple data series and a dropdown allowing us to change which trend line we displayed. We added a click event handler so that a new chart appeared with expanded data for the bar clicked on. We finished by adding hover event handlers to create a table of all the data points for the selected data series.

In the next chapter, we will look at stacked bar charts and horizontal bar charts. We will also look at additional style options to help in our understanding of the data.

4
Horizontal and Stacked Bar Charts

We have looked at line, area, and bar charts, and some of the limitations of these charts. We will start this chapter by looking at the best uses of horizontal and stacked bar charts. We will also learn how to hide different elements on our axes and modify our data point labels. The following topics will be covered in this chapter:

- Creating a basic horizontal chart
- Modifying our chart to be a stacked bar chart so that the data is easier to read
- Examining the ways to determine when and how to visualize data
- Removing grid lines and axis labels in an attempt to further customize our charts
- Overlaying a line on our chart to act as a threshold denoting business logic

Turning our chart on its side

We come to work on Thursday morning to find an e-mail from Sara waiting for us. "I liked the chart you did with some of our product categories," she says. "I'm sending over numbers for a few others and I'd like this chart to be broken out by months instead of quarters."

We start thinking through how to best represent this data. There are more data series, and the legend takes up space within the div element. This limits the space available to us for a vertical bar chart, so we decide on a horizontal bar chart. Horizontal bar charts are rotated 90 degrees; the x axis becomes the vertical axis, and the y axis is the horizontal axis. If any of our data series contain both x and y values, we will need to switch their order to `[[y, x], [y, x], [y,x]]`.

We open the spreadsheet Sara sent over. There are nine product categories to plot, with 12 data points per category. That's 108 bars on our graph. Even using a horizontal chart, it may be a tight fit. We decide to move forward and see what happens:

1. We include the same plugins as we included with the other bar graphs. This time, however, we also add `canvasAxisLabelRenderer` so that we can rotate the label on our *y* axis:

```
<script src="../js/jqplot.categoryAxisRenderer.min.js"></script>
<script src="../js/jqplot.barRenderer.min.js"></script>
<script src="../js/jqplot.canvasTextRenderer.min.js"></script>
<script src="../js/jqplot.canvasAxisTickRenderer.min.js"></script>
<script src="../js/jqplot.canvasAxisLabelRenderer.min.js"></
script>
<script>
```

2. We include the nine data arrays for our product categories. Since we are only including one axis value for our bar graphs, we don't have to switch the order of the x and y values:

```
$(document).ready(function(){
  var dvds = [151537.81, 141980.66, 126915.19, 96764.25,
152154.38, 130709.87, 120796.76, 111966.62, 86397.29, 74051.78,
67587.91, 83181.89];
  var cds = [176794.11, 165644.10, 148067.72, 112891.63,
152154.38, 143780.85, 140929.55, 130627.73, 100796.84, 86393.75,
78852.56, 97045.54];
  var tvs = [73633.00, 90200.42, 92964.15, 85527.02, 61356.34,
91614.46, 87949.88, 82453.01, 98218.97, 81849.15, 80212.16,
76345.37];
  var computers = [106196.16, 117995.73, 142713.61, 172020.86,
108309.43, 139166.61, 142894.28, 130468.69, 143960.95, 149959.33,
155957.70, 134764.98];
  var software = [150274.99, 139141.04, 124376.89, 90313.30,
178933.56, 133803.33, 112743.64, 104502.18, 60478.10, 41469.00,
35483.65, 43670.49];
  var digital = [26519.12, 26503.06, 23690.84, 22578.33, 23938.96,
27405.50, 28185.91, 26125.55, 40318.73, 44924.75, 43368.91,
53375.05];
  var consoles =[13962.94, 14237.89, 36609.86, 57494.22, 16792.64,
24069.15, 34096.61, 19356.21, 75174.26, 75775.12, 95298.26,
85518.01];
  var dvd_players = [7518.51, 7666.55, 19713.00, 30958.43,
9042.19, 12960.31, 18359.72, 10422.58, 18793.56, 18943.78,
23824.56, 21379.50];
  var media_streamers = [0, 0, 0, 0, 0, 0, 0, 0, 31322.61,
31572.97, 39707.61, 35632.50];
```

```
var ticks = ['Nov 2011', 'Dec 2011', 'Jan 2012', 'Feb 2012',
'Mar 2012', 'Apr 2012', 'May 2012', 'Jun 2012', 'Jul 2012', 'Aug
2012', 'Sep 2012', 'Oct 2012'];
```

3. We create our jqPlot object and pass in the nine data arrays. For this chart, we change the angle of our ticks to 15 degrees. This will make our axes a little more compact:

```
var rev_category = $.jqplot ('rev_category', [ dvds, cds,
software, digital, tvs, computers, consoles, dvd_players, media_
streamers],
  {
    title:'Monthly Revenue by Product Category',
    axesDefaults: {
      tickRenderer: $.jqplot.CanvasAxisTickRenderer,
      tickOptions: { angle: -15 }
    },
```

4. With the restraints of our large dataset, we need to save space where we can. We set the `shadow` option to `false`. In order to make our chart horizontal, we set `barDirection` to `horizontal` under `rendererOptions`. We also set `barMargin` and `barPadding` to `0`, so our bars will have a little more room to expand in the confines of our plot:

```
seriesDefaults: {
  renderer:$.jqplot.BarRenderer,
  shadow: false,
  rendererOptions: {
    barDirection: 'horizontal',
    barPadding: 0,
    barMargin: 0
  }
},
```

5. We noticed that the default series colors for jqPlot tend to blend together when our bars get very small. So, we pick nine colors that seem to have good contrast and set the `color` option for eight of our series. The default color for the seventh series works with our other colors, saving us from finding another color:

```
series: [
  { label: 'DVDs/Blu-ray', color: '#FF0000' },
  { label: 'Music CDs', color: '#0BBBE0' },
  { label: 'Software', color: '#0000FF' },
  { label: 'Digital', color: '#555' },
  { label: 'TVs', color: '#FF960C' },
  { label: 'Computers', color: '#00007F' },
```

```
        { label: 'Game Consoles', },
        { label: 'DVD Players', color: '#56C2B2' },
        { label: 'Media Streamers', color: '#62FF0D' },
    ],
    legend: {
        show: true,
        placement: 'outsideGrid',
        location: 'ne'
    },
```

6. Since our chart is horizontal, we need to switch the options for the two axes. We move what was the old *y* axis to be the *x* axis:

```
axes:{
    xaxis:{
        label: 'Revenue in Dollars',
        tickOptions: { formatString: "$%'d" }
    },
```

7. Normally, we would set the *x* axis to use our CategoryAxisRenderer, but for this chart we will change this to the *y* axis. Similar to how we set a renderer for our tick options, we pass the CanvasAxisLabelRenderer class to labelRenderer. By default, the angle of the label on the *y* axis will be 90 degrees, so we don't explicitly need to set an angle. If we do set it, we will set it under labelOptions:

```
        yaxis: {
            renderer: $.jqplot.CategoryAxisRenderer,
            label: 'Months',
            labelRenderer: $.jqplot.CanvasAxisLabelRenderer,
            ticks: ticks,
        }
    }
});
});
</script>
```

8. We finish our chart by increasing the height of the div that holds our plot. The default height for a plot is 400px, but we need it to be taller, so we set the height to 700px:

```
<div id="rev_category" style="width:700px;height:700px;"></div>
```

When we finish coding our plot, we load the new report in our browser. It appears we were overconfident about the abilities of a horizontal chart.

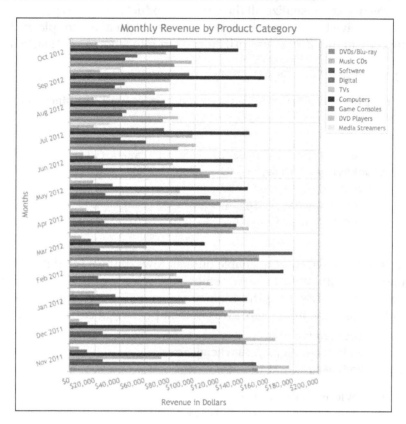

Using a stacked bar chart to make our data easier to read

There are just too many data points. Also, since the bars are so small, it is hard to compare one to another. We can increase the height of the chart, but the user will have to scroll up and down trying to compare different months.

This dead end is a good time for us to remember a tenet we learned as children. Granted, it was not taught to us in the framework of data visualization, but it still applies. "Just because we can, doesn't mean we should." With jqPlot, we can import any type of data and create many different chart types. We have to keep in mind the type of data we are representing. Stephen Few points out that we need to compare our data side by side (http://www.tableausoftware.com/blog/stephen-few-data-visualization). Expecting people to hold 108 bars in memory and comparing them will wear out a user.

Another tenet of Stephen Few is to present data in different ways to see it from different angles. Thinking along these lines, we decide we can create a stacked bar chart. This way, we can visualize all the various product categories per month, but we will only have twelve bars in our chart. We only need to make a couple of changes to our existing code to transform our horizontal chart into a horizontal stacked bar chart.

We start by opening up the code from the previous chart:

1. All the plugins and data series are the same. As with the stacked area charts, we set `stackSeries` to `true`.

```
{
  title:'Monthly Revenue by Product Category',
  stackSeries: true,
  axesDefaults: {
    tickRenderer: $.jqplot.CanvasAxisTickRenderer,
    tickOptions: { angle: -15 }
  },
```

2. For this chart, we want to enable our shadows, but we want the shadows to appear in a different place. We remove the `shadow` option and replace it with `shadowAngle`. By setting the angle to `135`, our shadows appear underneath our bars, as if the light source was in the upper-right corner of our plot:

```
seriesDefaults: {
  renderer:$.jqplot.BarRenderer,
  shadowAngle: 135,
```

3. In our previous chart, we turned off all padding and margins between our bars. Since we have more space, we add these back. Also, we set `shadowAlpha` to `0.1` to give our bars a little bit of shadow:

```
rendererOptions: {
  barDirection: 'horizontal',
  barPadding: 5,
  barMargin: 10,
  shadowAlpha: 0.1
}
},
```

4. Since the stacks for our chart will be larger, we remove the color settings for each series and use the default colors jqPlot provides:

```
series: [
    { label: 'DVDs/Blu-ray' },
    { label: 'Music CDs' },
    { label: 'Software' },
    { label: 'Digital' },
    { label: 'TVs' },
    { label: 'Computers' },
    { label: 'Game Consoles' },
    { label: 'DVD Players' },
    { label: 'Media Streamers' }
],
```

5. Next, we place the legend back inside our grid. We also add padding to the *x* axis so that the legend does not cover any of our bars:

```
legend: { show: true, placement: 'insideGrid', location: 'ne'
},
axes:{
    xaxis:{ label: 'Revenue in Dollars',
        padMax: 1.3
        tickOptions: { formatString: "$%'d" }
    },
    yaxis: {
        renderer: $.jqplot.CategoryAxisRenderer,
        label: 'Months',
        ticks: ticks
    }
}
});
});
</script>
```

6. We finish by decreasing the height of the chart div to `500px`:

```
<div id="rev_category" style="width:700px;height:500px;"></div>
```

In the following screenshot, we see the results of our work. This chart works much better.

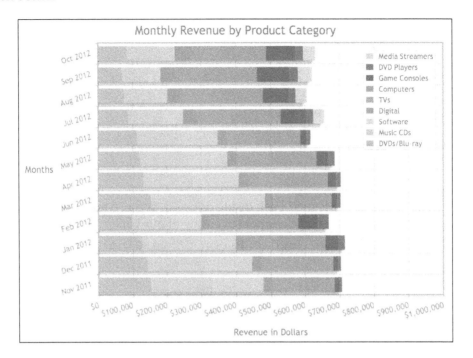

It's easier to see everything and it's possible to see trends in the data over the months. Also, we get a second benefit with a stacked bar chart; we can see the total revenue with all the bars stacked together.

Understanding the limits of data

This chart gets us thinking. Knowing how the VPs think, they might want to drill down into the data. We can implement an event handler for the `jqplotDataClick` event. The problem lies in the data to pull with this event.

We can load two different charts when the user clicks on one of the bar stacks. One option is to load a second chart with 12 months of data for the clicked product category. The other option is to load the monthly data of all the product categories for the bar representing the month clicked.

This is when more detail will help us. We need to talk to Sara and the other VPs. When we have a better understanding of the issues they want to explore, we can create better visualizations of the data. We call Calvin and ask him to come by to chat. About 10 minutes later, Calvin walks in. "So, what's up?" he asks.

We show him the new charts and explain our concerns. Some of our charts have way too many data points and there are so many directions we could go with visualizing the data. Calvin nods his head for a few seconds after we finish our explanation. "I completely understand. I think what you've done is great and will help them. I think another problem we have is that some people are already thinking about phase two."

Making our chart compact

He continues, "A few have talked about a dashboard. They want each VP and manager to see a quick snapshot of all the relevant data for their areas. As a first step, why don't I walk Sara through these new charts and explain your rationale behind the design decisions. Then, we'll see what she thinks."

Calvin sends us to lunch while he talks with Sara. When we get back, Calvin is waiting on us. "Good news," he says. "Sara is on board with what you have. She had the idea of tweaking the large horizontal chart to only show the past month's data for all product categories. As a test of the phase two dashboard, make it compact so that it fits on a page with several other charts."

We tell Calvin we should have it wrapped up this afternoon and get ready for the big meeting tomorrow. He nods and walks out. Taking our earlier chart from 108 bars down to only nine bars will be a lot easier to compress.

Removing axis labels and adding point labels

Since this chart will be in a confined space, we will turn off the ticks and label on the y axis to increase the amount of area in the chart. We will use the same plugins as before, but we will also include the `pointLabels` plugin this time:

1. Since this is a proof-of-concept chart, we just pass in the last month's data for each data series and wrap it in an array. If Sara signs off on this, we can create a data renderer to pull last month's data dynamically:

   ```
   . . .
   <script src="../js/jqplot.pointLabels.min.js"></script>
   . . .
     var rev_category = $.jqplot ('rev_category', [ [dvds[11]],
   [cds[11]], [software[11]], [digital[11]], [tvs[11]],
   [computers[11]], [consoles[11]], [dvd_players[11]], [media_
   streamers[11]]],
     . . .
   ```

2. Next, we use the new `edgeTolerance` option for the `pointLabels` option. In the previous charts, the point labels disappeared when they got too close to the edge of the plot. Our workaround was to add padding to the *y* axis. With `edgeTolerance`, if our point label is too long, it will continue beyond the edge of the plot. If it passes our newly set threshold, jqPlot will turn off the label:

```
seriesDefaults: {
  renderer:$.jqplot.BarRenderer,
  pointLabels: { show: true, edgeTolerance: -75 },
  rendererOptions: {
    barDirection: 'horizontal',
    barPadding: 10,
    barMargin: 10,
    shadow: false
  }
},
```

3. We can use text labels instead of the *y* value for our point labels. We do away with the legend and set `labels` to the category name for the `pointLabels` option. The `labels` option takes an array because it expects a label for each point on the data series. Since we only have one data point per series, our arrays will also have one element:

```
series: [
    { label: 'DVDs/Blu-ray', color: '#FF0000', pointLabels:{
labels:['DVDs/Blu-ray'] } },
    { label: 'Music CDs', color: '#0BBBE0', pointLabels:{
labels:['Music CDs'] } },
    { label: 'Software', color: '#0000FF', pointLabels:{
labels:['Software'] } },
    { label: 'Digital', color: '#555', pointLabels:{
labels:['Digital'] } },
    { label: 'TVs', color: '#FF960C', pointLabels:{
labels:['TVs'] } },
    { label: 'Computers', color: '#00007F', pointLabels:{
labels:['Computers'] } },
    { label: 'Game Consoles', pointLabels:{ labels:['Game
Consoles'] } },
    { label: 'DVD Players', color: '#56C2B2', pointLabels:{
labels:['DVDs/Blu-ray Players'] } },
    { label: 'Media Streamers', color: '#62FF0D', pointLabels:{
labels:['Media Streamers'] } },
  ],
```

4. We want to decrease the amount of space taken up by all the data on the *x* axis. So, we set `fontSize` to `10pt` for the *x* axis:

```
axes:{
  xaxis:{ label: 'Revenue in Dollars',
    tickOptions: {
      formatString: "$%'d",
      fontSize: '10pt'
    }
  },
```

5. We can explain the data on the *y* axis with the HTML title and our point labels; so, we can hide the ticks and axis label. The parts of our ticks we can turn off are the grid lines, marks, and labels. The corresponding options under `tickOptions` are `showGridline`, `showMark`, and `showLabel`. We want to turn off all three so we use `show` and set it to `false`. We hide the axis label by setting `showLabel` to `false`:

```
  yaxis: {
    renderer: $.jqplot.CategoryAxisRenderer,
    tickOptions: { show: false },
    showLabel: false
  }
}
});
});
</script>
```

6. We add a bit of HTML to give a heading to our new dashboard and chart. We also include some CSS to format our point labels to make them easier to read on our plot:

```
<h1>Dashboard</h1>
<div id="monthly_rev" class="dashboard block">
  <h2>Last Month's Revenue by Product Category</h2>
  <div id="rev_category" style="width:200px; height:400px;"></div>
</div>
<style>
.jqplot-point-label {
  font-size: .75em;
  z-index: 2;
  white-space: nowrap;
  border: 1.5px solid #aaaaaa;
  padding: 1px 2px;
  background-color: #eeccdd;
}
</style>
```

We load our new dashboard, and the chart works as we intended. The changes to our styles make the chart easier to view. Also, it is small enough, so we can place several other charts next to it, and it will all fit on one screen.

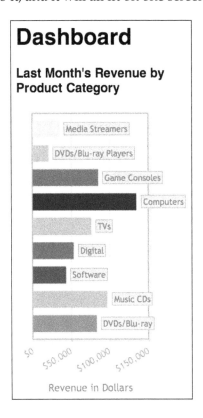

With our restrictions, we could not fit all these data series in a vertical bar chart, so this is one of the times that horizontal charts shine. Also, we see that most of our point labels stay inside our plot, but the label for **Computers** and **Game Consoles** extend beyond the chart. This is a compromise we made; either the labels extend beyond the chart or our bars are shorter and harder to see if we add padding.

As we think about what might come next, Calvin walks in the office with a woman. "This is Sara. She wanted to stop by and meet you two." We introduce ourselves and you mention that we just wrapped up the dashboard prototype.

Adding a threshold to our chart

Sara leans toward the screen, "This is exactly what we need. I'm already thinking that we need to put a line on here, like a threshold. One of our new initiatives is to examine the product categories we are in. If any category drops below monthly revenue of $50,000, it is flagged, and we will evaluate whether we need to stay in that category."

You mention that we can make the change quickly. We won't need to change much in our existing chart:

1. We start by including the `canvasOverlay` plugin:

    ```
    . . .
    <script src="../js/jqplot.canvasOverlay.min.js"></script>
    . . .
    ```

2. We create a `canvasOverlay` option and set `show` to `true`. Next, we create the `objects` option, which accepts an array of objects with the options for each line we want to draw. For each line, we have the four options of `verticalLine`, `dashedVerticalLine`, `horizontalLine`, and `dashedHorizontalLine`. For this chart, we create a `verticalLine` object:

    ```
    . . .
        canvasOverlay: {
          show: true,
          objects: [
            {
              verticalLine: {
    ```

3. We set `name` to `threshold` so that we have an easy way to access this line later. Since our threshold is `50000`, we set this as the x value. We set `lineWidth` to 2 to make it thicker, and we set `yOffset` to 0 so that our line will stretch all the way to the top and bottom of our chart.

    ```
                name: 'threshold',
                x: 50000,
                lineWidth: 2,
                color: '#373737',
                shadow: false,
                yOffset: 0
              }
            }
          ]
        },
        . . .
    ```

We load the new report for Sara and can immediately see that a few product categories are below the threshold.

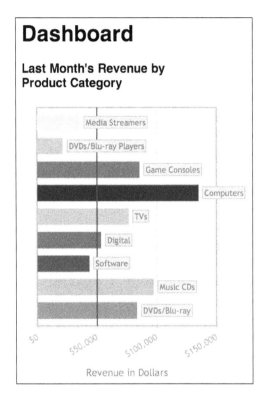

"Perfect," says Sara. "You do not understand how much these reports are going to help the management team. You are going to become everyone's new best friends after tomorrow's meeting." Calvin steps closer and interjects, "Sara, if you are happy with what we have, then we'll make them accessible for the presentation tomorrow." Sara nods and Calvin looks at us and continues, "Sara and I will go finalize everything for the presentation and leave you two to wrap up." Calvin and Sara leave and we start deploying all our charts to our production server.

Knowing that phase two of this project is going to be a dashboard, we know that there will be a desire for pie charts, and maybe, donut charts. Every manager loves pie charts. We'll wait until after the meeting to see what direction they take.

Learning questions

1. How do you format your x and y data points for a horizontal bar chart?

2. What option do you set to add a horizontal or vertical line on top of your chart?

3. How do you remove grid lines from a chart?

4. Where do you set point labels and in what format are they needed?

5. What are some limitations of both vertical and horizontal bar charts?

Summary

We created a very crowded horizontal chart with over 100 bars. The chart was unusable, so we took another look at the data and presented it as a stacked bar chart. We moved on to creating a more compact bar chart by removing ticks and the axis label. We added the category names to our point labels to make up for removing the tick labels. Also, we represented business logic by overlaying a line on our chart.

In the next chapter, we will bake up some charts by exploring pie charts and donut charts. We will also examine some of the reasons why people hate pie charts.

5
Pie Charts and Donut Charts

In this chapter, we will learn about the proper contexts for using pie and donut charts. We will also look at some of the limitations and critiques of these charts. Also, we will discuss the different ways to parse and collate the data we get from our remote feeds. In addition, we will cover the following topics:

- Creating a basic pie chart and sorting the data points in descending order
- Modifying the styles and options to make it more readable and usable
- Building a pie chart with empty wedges
- Constructing pie charts and moving the labels further from the center
- Designing a donut chart showing browser usage and sorting each segment in the inner ring in descending order

Limitations of pie charts

We come to work on Friday and play catch up on all our work that's been on hold. In the afternoon, we keep waiting for word from the manager's meeting, but nothing is sent across. Finally, around 5 o'clock, Calvin stops by.

"You two are officially rock stars. Everyone loved what you did. There were some uncomfortable moments after seeing some of the data points visualized, but that was the point of this project. I just wanted to update you real quick that we'll have a meeting on Monday about phase two. Management has lots of ideas."

9 o'clock Monday morning, we find ourselves in a conference room with Calvin, Sara, and a couple of other VPs and managers. Calvin starts to speak, "Good morning. I'm glad everyone is here. This is an exploratory meeting about phase two, the management dashboard. There were a lot of ideas thrown out during the meeting on Friday, and we wanted to take the time to distill those ideas down into something actionable. That's also why I invited the two developers who have worked on this project. I wanted their feedback on the best reporting options as we move forward."

Roshan, VP of Operations, speaks up, "We want to give our management team quick snapshots of where we stand. Pie charts will be good for this. I want to show how the percentage of revenue for each product category compares to the others. I also want a pie chart showing the divisional revenues as a percentage. Then, for each division, managers will see a pie chart with just their product categories."

Before we can interject, Jeff, VP of Information Systems, adds his comments. "From the IT side, we need a pie chart showing browser usage. Could it be one of those charts that looks like donut with the browsers listed on the outer ring and the versions are on the inner ring? This will help us as we move forward building our website and the features that we can offer. Many on the team believe we still need to support IE 7 and 8."

There is a lull in the conversation, so I take the chance to add my observations. "I think the idea of giving snapshots of the data is a great idea. I do have some reservations about using pie charts, though. In preparation for this meeting, I did some cursory research. The consensus is that pie charts are just bad in so many ways. I found several good articles by Steve Fenton on his blog, `http://stevefenton.co.uk`, discussing the different ways pie charts can incorrectly represent data."

Roshan tries to interrupt, but I continue, "There are chart types that are best used for certain types of data. We have already created a bar chart showing the revenue for each product category. We believe that a bar chart is better for comparing one product category to the other categories. Pie charts are really only good when comparing two or three categories. With eleven categories, the smallest pie pieces will be indistinguishable. Now, a pie chart of divisional revenues will be fine. There are only three divisions."

Roshan speaks again, "I appreciate your concerns, but we have already promised this to the management team. So, we just need to implement it." You and I share a look of resignation and fear. The meeting transitions into more business rules and logic.

Making a pie chart with many data points

After the meeting concludes, we head back to our office to try and make the best of a possibly bad situation. We talk it over and decide to start on the product category pie chart first.

We have been in talks with the IT department, and they have created more data feeds for us. The one we will use for this chart returns an array of arrays. Each array has two elements: the division and product category as a label and the revenue for the last month. Here is the data it returns:

```
[
["Electronics - Computers", 134764.98],
["Nerd Corral - Service", 103405.96],
["Media & Software - Music CDs", 97045.54],
["Electronics - Game Consoles", 85518.01],
["Media & Software - DVDs/Blu-ray", 83181.89],
["Electronics - TVs", 76345.37],
["Media & Software - Digital Media", 53375.05],
["Nerd Corral - Parts", 47002.71],
["Media & Software - Software", 43670.49],
["Electronics - Media Streamers", 35632.50],
["Electronics - DVD/Blu-ray Players", 21379.50]
]
```

1. We include the pieRenderer plugin and the functions.js file. We create the dataPull function to wrap the remote data in an array, and then return it to jqPlot. We have made an addition to our remoteDataCallback function. It now passes all the options passed in by jqPlot to the data callback method we created:

```
<script src="../js/jqplot.pieRenderer.min.js"></script>
<script src="../js/functions.js"></script>
<script>
function dataPull(remoteData,options) {
  return [remoteData];
}

$(document).ready(function(){
  var divisions = $.jqplot ('divisions', './data/last_month_
revenue.json',
    {
      title: 'Percentage of Revenue by Product Category',
```

2. We set the renderer to `PieRenderer`, and then move on to the `renderer` options. We want to show the data labels of our pie pieces. By default, the labels are set to `percent`, which shows the percentage. If we want to change the label type, we will set `dataLabels` to `label`, `value`, or an array of custom labels:

```
seriesDefaults: {
  renderer:$.jqplot.PieRenderer,
  rendererOptions: {
    showDataLabels: true,
```

3. Next, we set `startAngle` to `-90` so that our pie pieces start at 12 o'clock. Also, we set `dataLabelThreshold` to `0`. By default, jqPlot hides slices of less than three percent of the total pie area. This way, we will have labels for all of our wedges:

```
    startAngle: -90,
    dataLabelThreshold: 0
  }
},
```

4. We set `dataRenderer` to use our `remoteDataCallback` function, and then pass in the `dataPull` function name as an option to the data renderer. Finally, we place the legend below the chart:

```
dataRenderer: remoteDataCallback,
dataRendererOptions: { dataCallback: dataPull },
legend: { show: true, placement: 'outside', location: 's' },
});
```

5. In an effort to make the pie charts easier to understand, we create a callback for the `jqplotDataHighlight` event handler. When a user highlights a pie piece, we pass in the label and the actual dollar amount to a div we named `tooltip`. We use a new function, `numberWithCommas`, to format our numbers with thousands place separators:

```
$('#divisions').on('jqplotDataHighlight',
  function (ev, seriesIndex, pointIndex, data) {
    $('#tooltip').html(data[0]+' - $'+numberWithCommas(data[1].
toFixed(2)));
  }
);
$('#divisions').on('jqplotDataUnhighlight',
  function (ev, seriesIndex, pointIndex, data) {
    $('#tooltip').html('');
  }
);
});
</script>
```

6. We finish by writing some CSS rules to have `tooltip` appear on top of our plot just above the pie chart:

```
<div id="divisions" style="width:400px;height:300px;"></div>
<div id="tooltip"></div>
<style>
  .jqplot-table-legend.jqplot-table-legend-label { white-space:
nowrap;}
  #tooltip { float:left;position: absolute; top:52px;left:75px;}
</style>
```

We load the chart in our browser and see the following result. It is overwhelming!

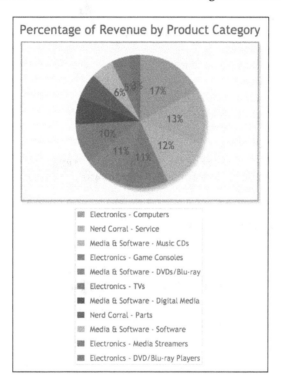

It's not as bad as we thought, but it can be better. We can see that one pie piece is so small that its label overlaps the label next to it. With others, the fill color is so dark that we can't make out the label unless we hover over the piece.

Also, there is the problem of trying to match the wedges to the legend. If we try to include the labels on the wedges, the chart will be unreadable. In its current form, if we want to know what product category has 10 percent of the total revenue, we have to count items in the legend till we find the category. We don't feel like the user will be able to compare categories quickly.

Styling our chart and adding functionality

We know that management wants these charts, so we will do our best with what we've got. We know we need to modify the fill color for our pie pieces. We also decide that we want to break our pieces apart.

We only need to add a couple of options to our existing chart. We set `sliceMargin` under `rendererOptions` to `5`, and this will break our pieces apart by 5 pixels. We also make use of the `seriesColors` option and pass in an array of hexadecimal color values. We finish by moving the legend to the left of the chart:

```
...
    seriesDefaults: {
      renderer:$.jqplot.PieRenderer,
      rendererOptions: {
        showDataLabels: true,
        startAngle: -90,
        dataLabelThreshold: 0,
        sliceMargin: 5
      }
    },
    seriesColors: [ "#4bb2c5", "#F4CA4A", "#EAA228", "#E4CAAB",
"#F47241", "#AED8D0", "#F2C185", "#FC4F4B", "#9B8DF4", "#00F41D",
"#988167" ],
...
legend: { show: true, placement: 'outside', location: 'e' },
...
```

With these updates, we reload the chart and see the results shown in the following screenshot. It's still an explosion of data and colors, but it's easier to read now:

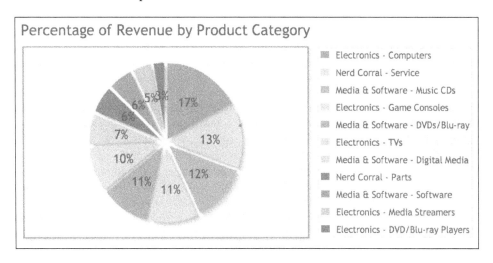

The labels are still mashed together and there are too many wedges. We can address our concerns with Calvin later.

Building a pie chart with empty wedges

With that out of the way, we move on to the pie chart showing revenue by division. There are only three data points, so it won't be as crammed. We use a different data source this time. We can see the results of the JSON feed in the following code:

```
{
  "Nerd Corral": {
    "Service": 103405.96,
    "Parts": 47002.71
  },
  "Media & Software": {
    "Music CDs": 97045.54,
    "DVDs/Blu-ray": 83181.89,
    "Digital Media": 53375.05,
    "Software": 43670.49
  },
  "Electronics": {
    "Computers": 134764.98,
    "Game Consoles": 85518.01,
    "TVs": 76345.37,
    "Media Streamers": 35632.50,
    "DVD/Blu-ray Players": 21379.50
  }
}
```

1. With this chart, we create a function to parse the JSON feed and break up the functionality into several functions. Our data renderer will call our new function, dataPull. It loops through each top-level property in the object:

   ```
   . . .
   <script>
   function dataPull(remoteData,options) {
     var data = new Array();
     var i = 0;
     for (var name in remoteData) {
   ```

2. We then pass the object to `calculate`. This function loops through all the child objects to calculate the total for the division. When `calculate` returns the total, we save it in an array with the division name as the label:

```
if (remoteData.hasOwnProperty(name)) {
  data[i] = [name, calculate(remoteData[name])];
  i++;
}
}
```

3. We want our array sorted in descending order based on total. We create a special function that the built-in `sort` method in JavaScript will use. Finally, we wrap our array in another array for jqPlot. With our `dataPull` function complete, we add our `calculate` function:

```
data.sort(descendingSort);
return [data];
}

function calculate(data)
{
  var total = 0;
  for (var name in data) {
    if (data.hasOwnProperty(name)) {
      total += data[name];
    }
  }
  return total;
}
```

4. Since we are passing an array to the built-in `sort` method, we create our own function called `descendingSort`. Normally, `sort` compares two strings. We will do so in our custom function, but we'll just compare the second elements of each array passed in as parameters:

```
function descendingSort(a, b) {
    if (a[1] === b[1]) return 0;
    if (a[1] < b[1]) return 1;
    return -1;
}
```

Some comparison functions will return `true` and `false`, or they will return `a-b` or `a+b`, but these return values can provide inconsistent results, and they do not match the ECMAScript specifications.

5. We want to turn off the fill for our pie pieces, so we set `fill` to `false` under `renderOptions`:

```
$(document).ready(function(){
  var divisions = $.jqplot ('divisions', './data/last_month_dept_
revenue.json',
    {
      title: "Last Month's Revenue by Division",
      seriesDefaults: {
        renderer:$.jqplot.PieRenderer,
        rendererOptions: {
          showDataLabels: true,
          sliceMargin: 4,
          fill: false,
          startAngle: -90
        }
      },
      seriesColors: [ "#FF0000", "#C2C250", "#0000FF"],
      dataRenderer: remoteDataCallback,
      dataRendererOptions: { dataCallback: dataPull },
```

6. We also want our legend to appear in one row. We set `renderOptions` under `legend`, and then set `numberRows` to 1:

```
      legend: {
        show: true,
        placement: 'outside',
        location: 's',
        rendererOptions: { numberRows: 1 }
      },
    });
  ...
```

Once we finish writing the code, we load the chart and see the result shown in the following screenshot. There is nothing groundbreaking about a pie chart with empty wedges, but there are advantages. The data is more prominent, without the user being overwhelmed by an array of colors. Also, we don't have to worry about the contrast between the color of the wedge and the color of the wedge label.

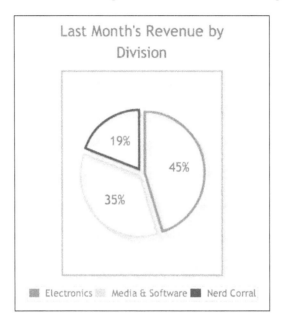

Creating a pie chart for each division with product category revenue

We decide that we will create all three divisional pie charts and place them side by side. This way, all the VPs will be able to compare each division. We do so by executing the following steps:

1. We start by repurposing our `dataPull` function. This time we make use of the `options` object passed into the function. We pass in the name of the division in `hashName`, which corresponds to an object in our JSON feed:

```
...
<script>
function dataPull(remoteData,options) {
  var obj = remoteData[options.hashName];
  var data = new Array();
  var ·i = 0;
```

2. We then loop through each child object in our divisional object. We build an array element for each product category with a label and the dollar value. Then, we wrap our data array in another array and return it to jqPlot:

```
for (var name in obj) {
    data[i] = [name, obj[name]];
    i++;
}
return [data];
}
```

3. For each chart, we use the same data feed. We decide to experiment with the padding setting under rendererOptions and seriesDefaults. For the first chart, we set padding to 0, so our pie chart should touch the edge of our plot. We also assign the division name to hashName under dataRendererOptions:

```
$(document).ready(function(){
    var nerd_corral = $.jqplot ('nerd_corral', './data/last_month_
dept_revenue.json',
    {
        title: "Nerd Corral",
        seriesDefaults: {
            renderer:$.jqplot.PieRenderer,
            rendererOptions: { showDataLabels: true, startAngle: -90,
padding: 0 }
        },
        seriesColors: [ "#00417F", "#0083FF"],
        dataRenderer: remoteDataCallback,
        dataRendererOptions: { dataCallback: dataPull, hashName: "Nerd
Corral" },
        legend: { show: true, placement: 'outside', location: 's' },
    });
```

4. Since the chart for **Electronics** has a few more data series, and the data labels tend to bunch up, we will use the dataLabelNudge option. A positive number moves the label away from the center of the pie, and a negative number moves it closer to the pie. We set it to 15. This way the label should stay within the wedge. We also set padding to 5 to give this pie chart a little bit of space from the edge, but not as much as by default:

```
var electronics = $.jqplot ('electronics', './data/last_month_
dept_revenue.json',
    {
        title: "Electronics",
        seriesDefaults: {
```

```
    renderer:$.jqplot.PieRenderer,
    rendererOptions: { showDataLabels: true, startAngle: -90,
dataLabelNudge: 15, padding: 5 }
   },
   seriesColors: [ "#7F0500", "#FF5F59", "#7F504E", "#CC0800",
"#382F2F"],
   dataRenderer: remoteDataCallback,
   dataRendererOptions: { dataCallback: dataPull, hashName:
"Electronics" },
   legend: { show: true, placement: 'outside', location: 's' },
  });
```

5. The settings for the **Media & Software** chart are almost identical. We don't enable `dataLabelNudge` on this chart, but we increase the `padding` option to `10`. By default, `padding` is set to `20`:

```
var media = $.jqplot ('media', './data/last_month_dept_revenue.
json',
  {
   title: "Media & Software",
   seriesDefaults: {
    renderer:$.jqplot.PieRenderer,
    rendererOptions: { showDataLabels: true, startAngle: -90,
padding: 10 }
   },
   seriesColors: [ "#007F19", "#69FF86", "#6B7F6F", "#A1BFA7"],
   dataRenderer: remoteDataCallback,
   dataRendererOptions: { dataCallback: dataPull, hashName:
"Media & Software" },
   legend: { show: true, placement: 'outside', location: 's' },
  });
});
</script>
```

6. With our other pie charts, it was hard to read the labels on the dark-colored wedges. We set the CSS to make the labels white with some text shadow:

```
<div id="nerd_corral" style="width:200px;height:200px;float:le
ft;"></div>
<div id="electronics" style="width:200px;height:200px;float:le
ft;"></div>
<div id="media" style="width:200px;height:200px;float:left;"></
div>
<style>.jqplot-pie-series.jqplot-data-label { color: #fff; text-
shadow: 2px 2px 2px #000;}</style>
```

With all of this coded, we load the charts in our browser and see the following results:

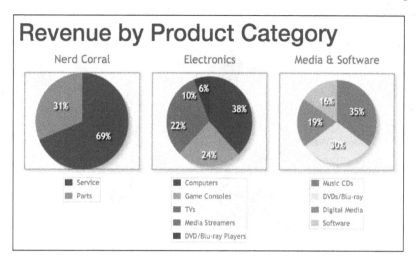

The middle chart, with a little bit of padding, looks as good along with the nudged data labels. We take a closer look at the charts and notice they demonstrate the good and bad elements of pie charts.

The chart for the Nerd Corral division has only two data points. This is when pie charts shine, comparing one element against the total. If there was a divisional directive that revenue from parts should never exceed 40 percent, then a manager could very quickly see where they stand. The other two charts are harder to compare. Another weakness of pie charts is that they are "snapshots"; they don't show trending over time. Also, pie charts don't provide enough data.

Calvin stops by as we are wrapping up for lunch. We show him the charts we created this morning and share our concerns with him. "I get it. Seeing these charts with live data makes your point stronger. Unfortunately, you might still have to put these charts into production. In the end, the management team has the final decision. Hey, why don't we head to lunch, and after you finish the chart for IT, we'll have a follow-up meeting to present what you have. Then, we'll talk about alternate solutions."

Defining donut charts

We get back from lunch and start working on the donut chart for Jeff. As we look at the options for donut charts, we realize that people use different names and definitions for donut charts. Some say a donut chart is simply a pie chart with a hole in the middle of it. Others call it a ring chart. Some types of donut or ring charts have concentric circles of data. These charts group data in the inner circles to correspond to data in the outer ring with matching colored wedges.

The following screenshot shows what Jeff expects:

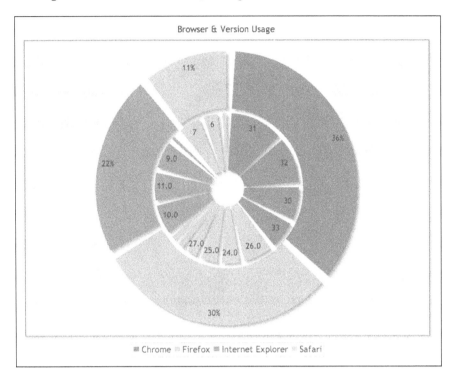

Building a donut chart to show web browser usage

We find the data feed, and it is composed of nested objects. We'll need to manipulate the remote data quite a bit to get it in the format we need. We achieve this by executing the following steps:

1. We start by including the `donutRenderer` plugin file. With donut charts, we can use `seriesColors` for each ring, so we create `arrSeriesColors` to store the colors of our outer rings. Then, we create `innerRingColors` to hold the matching colors for our inner ring wedges:

    ```
    <script src="../js/jqplot.donutRenderer.min.js"></script>
    <script src="../js/functions.js"></script>
    <script>
    var arrSeriesColors = "#4bb2c5", "#F4CA4A", "#EAA228", "#E4CAAB",
    "#00CC55", "#AED8D0", "#F2C185"];
    var innerRingColors = [];
    ```

2. Next, we create our function to parse our remote data. Since we have multiple levels in our JSON, we decide to store the `browsers` and `versions` objects in variables to make our code a little easier to read. We pass the browser data to our `parseBrowsers` function and do the same for our version data with `parseVersions`. Once all the data is processed, we put it in `data` and return it to jqPlot:

```
function dataPull(remoteData,options) {
  var data = [];
  var b = remoteData.browsers, v = remoteData.versions;

  var browser = parseBrowsers(b);
  var version = parseVersions(v,browser);
  data = [browser, version];
  return data;
}
```

3. The `parseBrowsers` function does the same thing as our other functions that looped through the first level of our JSON object. We grab each name, and we add this and the number of visits to our data array. When we're done, we sort the array, and then pass back the browser data to `dataPull`:

```
function parseBrowsers(b) {
  var browsers = [], i = 0;
  for (var name in b) {
    if (b.hasOwnProperty(name)) {
      browsers[i] = [name, b[name]];
      i++;
    }
  }
  browsers.sort(descendingSort);
  return browsers;
}
```

4. Our `parseVersions` function is a bit more detailed. First, we pass in both the versions data and the new `browser` array. We start by looping through our `browser` array. We then use the name to find the corresponding object in our versions object:

```
function parseVersions(v,browser) {
  var versions = [], i = 0;
  for(i=0;i<browser.length;i++){
    var name = browser[i][0];
```

5. We create a temporary array to hold all the data points for each browser. Then, we loop through each element in the chosen browser and add them to the `innerRing` array. We also add the browser name as the third element in our data point array. With this done, we'll be able to add the browser to our tooltip later:

```
var innerRing = [];
if (v.hasOwnProperty(name)) {
  for (var ver in v[name]) {
    innerRing.push([ver, v[name][ver], name]);
```

6. Once we add the data, we find the corresponding color in `arrSeriesColors` and add it to `innerRingColors`. This way, the version wedge color will match the color of the browser it belongs to:

```
    innerRingColors.push(arrSeriesColors[i]);
  }
}
```

7. Once we have looped through all the versions for the current browser, we sort `innerRing`. Then, we loop through `innerRing` and add the elements to our `versions` array. This way, all the version wedges will be next to the browser wedge in the outer ring, and they will be arranged in descending order:

```
innerRing.sort(descendingSort);
for(var j=0;j<innerRing.length;j++){
  versions.push(innerRing[j]);
  }
 }
 return versions;
}
```

8. After we complete the data parsing, we move on to setting up our graph. We set `renderer` to `DonutRenderer`. For this chart, we add in a couple of other renderer options. We set `innerDiameter` to `50` so that our inner ring will be wider to accommodate our labels. We also assign our `arrSeriesColors` array to `seriesColors`:

```
$(document).ready(function(){
  var browser_plot = $.jqplot ('browser_plot', './data/browser_
stats.json',
  {
    title: 'Web Browser Usage',
    seriesDefaults: {
      renderer:$.jqplot.DonutRenderer,
      rendererOptions: {
        showDataLabels: true,
        sliceMargin: 4,
```

```
        startAngle: -90,
        innerDiameter: 50,
        dataLabelThreshold: 0
      }
    },
  seriesColors: arrSeriesColors,
```

9. The `seriesColors` option is available within each series, so for our inner ring we assign it `innerRingColors` so our wedges will match the outer ring. Since our inner ring will not appear on the legend, we will override the series defaults and set `dataLabels` to `label`. Also, we move the inner ring labels closer to the outer edge by setting `dataLabelPositionFactor` to `.75`. This option takes a percentage as a decimal, whereas `dataLabelNudge` uses actual pixel values. So, with `dataLabelPositionFactor`, the position of our labels will scale if we change the size of our chart:

```
    series: [
      { },
      {
        seriesColors: innerRingColors,
        rendererOptions: {
          dataLabels: 'label',
          dataLabelPositionFactor: .75
        }
      }
    ],
```

10. We use the same options as our other charts for the data renderer and legend options:

```
    dataRenderer: remoteDataCallback,
    dataRendererOptions: { dataCallback: dataPull },
    legend: {
      show: true,
      placement: 'outside',
      location: 's',
      rendererOptions: { numberRows: 1 }
    },
  });
```

11. Next, we make use of the `jqplotDataHighlight` event. We want to display the percentage of usage as well as the browser and version names in our tooltip for our inner ring:

```
    $('#browser_plot').on('jqplotDataHighlight',
      function (ev, seriesIndex, pointIndex, data) {
        var total = 0;
```

12. We need to calculate the percentage for the wedge that is highlighted. This means we need to loop through the `series` data array for the highlighted series to get our total:

```
for(var i=0;i<browser_plot.series[seriesIndex].data.
length;i++) {
    total += browser_plot.series[seriesIndex].data[i][1];
}
```

13. Next, we calculate the percentage, and then we add the value to our tooltip. Since our outer ring does not have the third element in its data array, we add an `if` statement to only display the browser and percentage:

```
var percent = data[1] / total;
percent = percent * 100;
if(seriesIndex == 0) {
  $('#tooltip').html(data[0]+' - '+percent.toFixed(2)+'%');
} else {
  $('#tooltip').html(data[2]+': '+data[0]+' - '+percent.
toFixed(2)+'%');
    }
  }
);
```

14. We clear the tooltip with the `jqplotDataUnhighlight` event:

```
$('#browser_plot').on('jqplotDataUnhighlight',
  function (ev, seriesIndex, pointIndex, data) {
    $('#tooltip').html('');
  }
  );
});
</script>
```

15. We finish the chart by increasing the width and height so that all the wedges are large enough to hold the labels:

```
<div id="browser_plot" style="width:800px;height:600px;margin-
left:30px;"></div>
<div id="tooltip"></div>
<style>
  .jqplot-table-legend.jqplot-table-legend-label { white-space:
nowrap; padding:3px;}
  .jqplot-table-legend { padding: 3px; font-size: 1.25em;}
  .jqplot-donut-series.jqplot-data-label { color: #fff; text-
shadow: 2px 2px 2px #000;}
  #tooltip { float:left;position: absolute; top:50px;left:100px;}
</style>
```

Once we complete our coding, we load the chart in our browser. We can see the results in the following screenshot. The chart matches what we originally conceived. Jeff should be happy!

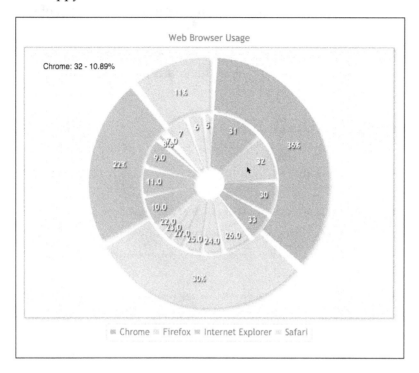

We notice that one of the slices is so small that it isn't rendered even with `dataLabelThreshold` set to `0`. Counting all the percentages of the inner ring, we determine that the percentage for Internet Explorer 7.0 is less than 1 percent. For our purposes, missing 1 percent will not make a huge difference.

Calvin stops by a few minutes later and we show him what we have. "Good work, let me call around and try and set up a quick meeting." Calvin steps out of the room, and 20 minutes later, we are sitting in the same conference room as this morning.

We walk them through the charts we created. When we show them the product category chart, Jeff says, "wow, that is a lot of data." After some discussion, everyone agrees that the product category chart is overwhelming. We decide we'll revisit the chart later.

They really like the divisional revenue chart. Someone mentions that the Nerd Corral chart works well, but the others are a bit jumbled. Finally, we show off Jeff's chart. Jeff likes it, especially since it shows that traffic for Internet Explorer 7 and 8 is not very high. We suggest it might work just as well as a bar chart.

Roshan speaks up, "I really like what you two have done. After seeing the charts, we have to agree with you on some of your concerns. I think the next step will be to take the charts you created and make them more interactive. When I move my mouse over a data point, can the data appear near my cursor instead of somewhere else on the page?"

We tell Roshan we should be able to do that. We head back to our office and gather our things to head home. We'll start on making the charts more interactive tomorrow.

Learning questions

1. What option did we set to customize the colors of our pie pieces?
2. If our data labels are bunched together, what option can we set to make them easier to read?
3. What are the three types of labels we can display for our wedges?
4. How did we get our legend to display in a single line?
5. What were some of the limitations or problems with pie charts that we discussed?
6. What is a better way to display browser usage data, but still use a pie chart?
7. As an experiment, we want to group all the products by division in our "Percentage of Revenue by Product Category" chart. We also want all products in the same division colored the same. How would we accomplish this?

Summary

We looked at the best uses of pie and donut charts. We also discussed the disadvantages of using these chart types. We looked at some ways to add functionality to a pie or donut chart to lessen some of the issues. We learned the different ways to move data labels around.

We also learned how to create empty pie pieces and split these pieces apart. We covered how to sort our data points to make the charts easier to read. We developed different functions to parse our remote data.

In the next chapter, we will look at the cursor and highlighter plugins. We will also look at some of the animation options.

6
Spice Up Your Charts with Animation, Tooltips, and Highlighting

In the last five chapters, we have looked at how to create line charts, area charts, bar charts, pie charts, and donut charts. Now, we will look at ways to extend the functionality of our charts and how to make them easier to use. In this chapter, we will cover the following topics:

- Adding the cursor plugin and being able to see the data where our cursor is
- Making the tooltip follow our cursor and adding lines to make the cursor easier to follow
- Connecting the cursor with the legend and showing data points when our cursor intersects a data point
- Adding the highlighter plugin so that we only see data when we highlight a data point
- Extending the highlighter plugin to select a legend item
- Animating a line chart
- Augmenting the animation for a bar chart by varying the speed of the animations

Using the cursor plugin to see the data behind our charts

We return to our office on Tuesday morning and spend the first half of our morning reviewing the charts we have created so far. Calvin swings by, and we ask him for some direction on how to proceed.

"Well, I think Roshan's suggestion to show the coordinates at the point of the cursor will be a great starting point. Just experiment. You've proven that you can meet the requirements. Now, you need to make it easier for the management to digest the data you are presenting. I hate to say it, but if you can work in some eye candy to grab their attention, that will impress them all the more. The data should speak for itself, but sometimes, you need to glitz it up."

Calvin leaves and we pull out our earlier line chart, `1168_01_04.html`, showing profit and revenue on the same *y* axis. Since the data points for each line are so far apart, it is hard to get a good idea of what the actual dollar amounts are:

1. We start by including the cursor plugin file. Our original chart did not have a legend, so we add in labels for each data series and add options for our legend:

   ```
   <script src="../js/jqplot.cursor.min.js"></script>
   . . .
           series:[
             { label: 'Revenue' },
             { label: 'Profit' }
           ],
           legend: {
             show: true,
             placement: 'outsideGrid'
           },
   ```

2. To add the cursor, we create a `cursor` option and set the `show` option inside to `true`. Just as with the legend, we can position the tooltip showing our data points. There are eight possible locations based on the compass directions n, ne, e, se, s, sw, w, and nw. Using sw will place the tooltip in the lower-left corner:

   ```
           cursor: {
             show: true,
             tooltipLocation:'sw'
           },
           . . .
   ```

We load the chart in our browser and move our cursor around the chart. We move our cursor over the data point on our **Revenue** line for June and see that the total revenue for this month was **$752,294**. We also notice that the cursor tooltip uses the same format as our axes.

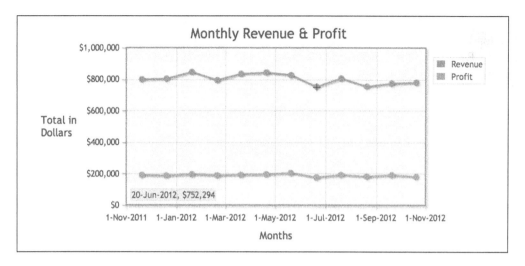

Making the tooltip follow the mouse and adding cursor lines

This is a nice addition to our chart, but we know that Roshan specifically asked for the tooltip to appear near his cursor. We also take Calvin's advice about making things a bit more engaging and easier to use.

We can enable lines to span the length of the grid and intersect with the cursor. This will make it more obvious where the user's cursor is on the grid. We can also use `tooltipLocation` to move our tooltip around respective to the cursor. We return to the chart we just created and make a few changes. We set the following options within the `cursor` object:

1. We start by changing `tooltipLocation` to `se`:

    ```
    cursor: {
      show: true,
      tooltipLocation:'se',
    ```

2. Next, we add the `followMouse` option and set it to `true` to allow the tooltip to follow the cursor:

    ```
    followMouse: true,
    ```

3. We enable both the vertical and horizontal cursor lines by setting
showVerticalLine and showHorizontalLine to true:

```
    showVerticalLine: true,
    showHorizontalLine: true
},
```

We load our updated chart and move our cursor to the data point for June 20 on our **Revenue** line. Looking at the following screenshot, we can see that revenue was **$752,294**:

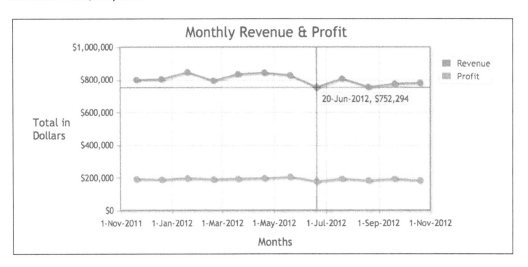

Pushing the limits of the cursor plugin

We decide to try the cursor plugin on a chart with multiple *y* axes. We pull up our profit and revenue chart with two *y* axes found in 1168_01_06.html. We copy the cursor options from the last chart. This time, we set the position of the tooltip to sw. We also remove the settings of the horizontal cursor line and leave only the vertical line:

```
cursor: {
    show: true,
    tooltipLocation:'sw',
    followMouse: true,
    showVerticalLine: true
},
```

We load the chart and move our cursor to November 20 on the **Profit** line. As we can see in the following screenshot, the tooltip overlaps our axis labels. This is something we need to remember as we move forward. With the tooltip following the cursor, it might extend beyond our chart, covering axis labels and other chart elements.

We also notice that with the revenue and profit lines so close together, it becomes hard to read the tooltip as we move our cursor around. We remove the `followMouse` option so that the tooltip will appear in the bottom-right corner of the chart:

```
cursor: {
    show: true,
    tooltipLocation:'sw',
    showVerticalLine: true
},
```

We can see the result in the following screenshot. Now, we can see our cursor interacting with the data point for each *y* axis. Also, we can read the data in the tooltip because it does not overlap labels or ticks.

Connecting the cursor with the legend

As we experiment, we come across the option to pass the data points from the cursor tooltip to the legend. We revisit the chart we just worked on, and save it as a new file, `1168_06_05.html`:

1. We include the canvas plugins so that we can rotate our ticks and labels. We need to do this since our legend will be taking up more space than normal:

   ```
   <script src="../js/jqplot.cursor.min.js"></script>
   <script src="../js/jqplot.canvasTextRenderer.min.js"></script>
   <script src="../js/jqplot.canvasAxisTickRenderer.min.js"></script>
   <script src="../js/jqplot.canvasAxisLabelRenderer.min.js"></script>
   ```

2. We set `showTooltip` to `false` so that we don't show data points in multiple places. We set `showVerticalLine` to `true`. By connecting the cursor to the legend, values will only appear when the cursor crosses data points. When our vertical line crosses a data point, the values will appear in the legend. So, `showVerticalLine` must be set in order for this to work:

   ```
   cursor: {
       show: true,
       showTooltip: false,
       showVerticalLine: true,
   ```

3. We set the new option, `showCursorLegend`, to `true`. By default, the format string for the cursor legend is `%s x:%s, y:%s`. We just want the label and the dollar amount. Since the label, the x value, and the y value are passed in this order, we wrap the date in a span to hide it when it is displayed:

   ```
       showCursorLegend: true,
       cursorLegendFormatString: '%s <span class="hidden">%s</span><span class="right">%s</span>'
   },
   . . .
   ```

4. Next, we set `labelRenderer` under `axesDefaults`, so it will affect all the axes:

   ```
   axesDefaults: {
     labelRenderer: $.jqplot.CanvasAxisLabelRenderer
   },
   axes:{
   . . .
   ```

5. Finally, we create several CSS styles for the legend. We give fixed widths to the table cells so that they don't expand and contract as we move the cursor:

```
<div id="revenueProfitChart" style="width:750px;"></div>
<style>
table.jqplot-legend {
   right: -65px;
   min-width: 165px;
}
table.jqplot-legend td { border: 0;}
td.jqplot-cursor-legend-swatch { width: 24px;}
td.jqplot-cursor-legend-label { padding-left: 10px;}
td.jqplot-cursor-legend-label .right {
   float:right;
   padding-right: 10px;
}
</style>
```

We move our cursor over April, and though the cursor is not actually on the data points, the vertical line intersects the points. We can see that our legend shows the dollar amount for each data point in April in the following screenshot:

We have created several charts using the cursor plugin in different ways. We'll let Roshan and the rest of the management team try them out and see which works best for them.

Using the highlighter plugin

We move on to the highlighter plugin. This plugin works very much like the cursor plugin, but it only highlights the data point that our cursor is hovering over. We will start with the **Social Media Shares** chart from *Chapter 2, More Line Charts, Area Charts, and Scatter Plots*, found in `1168_02_01.html`, which we created last week. There are a lot of data points to test with:

1. We start by including the highlighter plugin file with the other included JavaScript files:

```
<script src="../js/jqplot.dateAxisRenderer.min.js"></script>
<script src="../js/jqplot.highlighter.min.js"></script>
```

2. We will only add the `highlighter` option to our chart. No other change to the chart is necessary. As with the cursor plugin, we set `show` to `true` to enable the highlighter plugin. We want a halo to appear around the data point when we highlight it, so we set `showMarker` to `true`:

```
highlighter: {
    show: true,
    showMarker: true,
```

> Non-rendering plugins such as highlighter, cursor, or trend line are disabled by default to avoid possible conflicts with custom plugins. As we discussed, we can manually enable each plugin using the `show` option. If we are certain that there are no conflicts with our plugins, we can use the following shortcut:
>
> `$.jqplot.config.enablePlugins = true;`
>
> We set this option before we create our chart, and all non-renderers will be enabled.

3. As with the cursor plugin, there is a `tooltipLocation` option and eight possible positions. For this chart, we set `tooltipLocation` to `e` so that the tooltip appears to the right of our cursor. Finally, we set `tooltipAxes` to `yx`. This will place the `y` value first and the `x` value second, and separate them both by a comma:

```
    tooltipLocation: 'e',
    tooltipAxes: 'yx'
},
```

The other options for `tooltipAxes` are x, y, and xy (note that both can also be used in place of xy). We can use `formatString` to modify the entire tooltip, but the values will appear in the order specified in `tooltipAxes`.

We load the chart in our browser. As shown in the following screenshot, when we highlight a data point, the point appears larger, and a tooltip appears next to it:

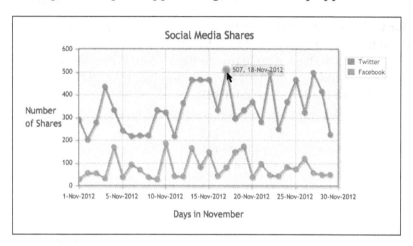

Extending the highlighter plugin to the legend

We can also use the highlighter on bar charts. We decide we will add the highlighter plugin to our stacked bar chart, **Monthly Revenue by Product Category**, from *Chapter 4, Horizontal and Stacked Bar Charts*, executing the following steps:

1. We use the same options as our **Social Media Shares** chart to which we added the highlighter plugin. However, in this chart, we decide to turn off the halo on the data point; so, we set `showMarker` to `false`. We also only want the x value. So, we set `tooltipAxes` to x:

```
. . .
    highlighter: {
      show: true,
      tooltipLocation: 'e',
      showMarker: false,
      tooltipAxes: 'x'
    },
. . .
```

2. We will also experiment and highlight the corresponding legend item when we highlight a bar. We'll do that by creating an event handler for `jqplotDataHighlight`. If we move our cursor from one stack to another within the same bar, `jqplotDataUnhighlight` will not fire. So, we begin by removing the `highlight` class from all the legend table rows:

```
$('#rev_category').on('jqplotDataHighlight',
    function (ev, seriesIndex, pointIndex, data) {
        $("tr.jqplot-table-legend").removeClass("highlight");
```

3. Our table has the last item of the data series at the top, so the legend items are in the opposite order of the data series. We use the `reverse` method, and then loop through each table row in the legend. When the index of the legend matches the index of the series we highlighted, we add the `highlight` class, which adds a border to the table cell:

```
$($("tr.jqplot-table-legend").get().reverse())
.each(function(i,index) {
  if(i == seriesIndex){
    $(this).addClass("highlight");
  }
});
});
```

4. For the `jqplotDataUnhighlight` event, we remove the `highlight` class from all our legend rows. Then, within our `style` element, we include the `highlight` class:

```
$('#rev_category').on('jqplotDataUnhighlight',
    function (ev, seriesIndex, pointIndex, data) {
        $("tr.jqplot-table-legend").removeClass("highlight");
});
...
<style>
.jqplot-highlighter-tooltip { background: rgba(208,208,208,1);}
.highlight .jqplot-table-legend-label { border: 1px solid #000;
padding: 0px 0px 0px 4px;}
</style>
```

We pull up the chart in our browser and see the results of our effort in the following screenshot. We begin highlighting different stacks in our bar chart. We are able to see the individual dollar amount for each data point. Also, the legend is highlighted so that it's easier to match a bar with the product category.

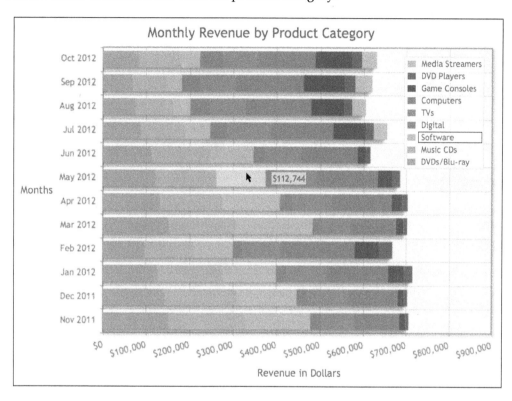

Animating line charts

We have completed our experiments with the cursor and highlighter plugins. Now, we'll try and add some eye candy to our reports. We take our **Social Media Shares** chart used earlier in the chapter and add one line to the plot: `animate: true`. This will cause the lines to load from left to right:

```
...
title:'Social Media Shares',
animate:true,
dataRenderer: remoteDataSource,
...
```

We load the updated chart and see the animation run:

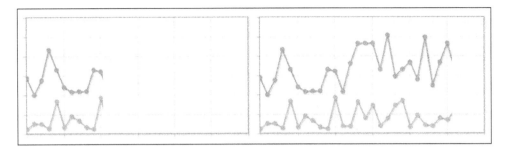

Animating bar charts with varying speeds

We can use the animation option with bar charts as well. With bar charts, the lines will load from the bottom and move upward. We pull our chart, **Quarterly Revenue by Product**, from *Chapter 3, Bar Charts and Digging into Data*, found in `1168_03_03.html`:

1. We start by setting the `animate` option to `true`:

   ```
   title:'Quarterly Revenue by Product',
   animate: true,
   axesDefaults: {
   ...
   ```

2. We can also set the speed for how fast each bar or line is animated. By default, each bar will start at the same speed, but we want the taller bars to move faster so that it gives the appearance that each bar finishes around the same time. To set the speed for each bar individually, we need to create a `rendererOptions` object within each series object. Next, we create an `animation` object, and then we set `speed`. For **DVDs/Blu-ray** and **Computers**, we vary the speed so that these bars load faster than the other two:

   ```
   ...
   series: [
     { label: 'DVDs/Blu-ray',
       rendererOptions: { animation: { speed: 1800 } }
     },
     { label: 'Music CDs',
       rendererOptions: { animation: { speed: 2200 } }
     },
     { label: 'TVs',
       rendererOptions: { animation: { speed: 2200 } }
     },
   ```

```
        { label: 'Computers',
          rendererOptions: { animation: { speed: 1800 } }
        }
    ],
    ...
```

When we load the chart in our browser, we see how the animation plays out; instead of each bar starting at the same height, they represent their different heights throughout the animation.

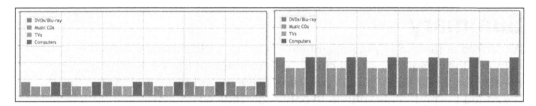

We finish this and notice we missed lunch. We e-mail Calvin to tell him we're going to lunch, and we'd like Sara to take a look and get her feedback.

When we get back from lunch, Sara and Calvin are waiting in our office. "I'm excited to see what you two have come up with," Sara says. We start with the cursor plugin. "I like these, especially the one that shows the values in the legend. Is it just me or are the numbers not completely accurate?" We confirm her suspicion. Even when the cursor is over a data point, it does not highlight the data point. Therefore, two users can get different numbers for the same data point, depending on where the cursor is positioned.

We move on to the highlighter plugin. "Yeah, I think this will be more useful for us. Can you make the background of the tooltip less transparent? This might make it easier to use. Also, I love the tooltips on the bar chart and the way the legend is highlighted."

We finish by showing her the animations. "These are cool. They might not be very useful, but they're fun, so leave them in."

Sara leans back in her chair. "I would love for you two to sit in on our meeting tomorrow. We have a new initiative related to the stock market, and I think you can help us present all the data in a different way."

Sara stands to leave. "I'm serious when I say this, you two are blowing peoples' minds with all this. I'll see you at 10 tomorrow morning." She and Calvin walk out and leave us to ponder the nature of this new "initiative".

Learning questions

1. What is the hierarchy to set the animation speed for a data series?

2. What additional option must be set to connect the cursor plugin with the legend?

3. Where can the tooltip be placed when using the cursor plugin?

4. With the highlighter plugin, what are the options to format `tooltipAxes`?

Summary

We looked at the cursor plugin, and we made our tooltip remain stationary as well as follow the cursor. We added cursor lines to pinpoint the location of the cursor. We also made the cursor plugin pass data to the legend instead of the tooltip. We added the highlighter plugin to only show data when a data point is selected.

Later, we experimented by highlighting a legend item when a data point was highlighted. We finished by animating a line chart and setting different animation speeds for a bar chart.

In the next chapter, we will look at OHLC and candlestick charts, which are used to display stock prices. We'll also make use of the highlighter plugin again.

Stock Market Charts – OHLC and Candlestick Charts

So far, we have created line charts and looked at various plugins to extend the functionality of our charts. Now, we will move on to OHLC and candlestick charts, which are used to visualize stock prices. We will also use several of the plugins we learned about in the last chapter to make our charts more interactive. In this chapter, we will cover the following topics:

- Gaining an understanding of the parts and using OHLC and candlestick charts
- Building an OHLC chart with last quarter's stock data and using the highlighter plugin to show all the data points
- Building a candlestick chart with the last 14 days of data
- Adding the cursor plugin to allow us to zoom in on a colored candlestick chart
- Creating canvas overlay lines using dates and adding tooltips to the lines
- Adding values to our remote data array, and then skipping some of those values when we create our tooltip

Looking at the employee stock option plan

On Tuesday morning, we show up for our 10 o'clock meeting. Roshan, Sara, and several other executives are there. A few minutes later, Roshan stands and starts the meeting. "I want to start by introducing Bob Albricht. He is a financial consultant helping us create our employee stock option plan. Remember, these meetings are privileged and not to be discussed until we make a public announcement."

We look at each other and shrug. Roshan continues, "Today we're discussing how to best communicate the benefits of this new program to our employees." I raise my hand, "Roshan, what do we contribute to this meeting?"

Roshan smiles, "Well, we want a stock chart on the dashboard you are creating. This way, the company's performance will be in front of everyone when they log in."

I ask, "Can't we just use a line chart?" Bob speaks up, "You can use a line chart, but it might be better to use an OHLC chart or a candlestick chart." Bob looks at Roshan and motions to the whiteboard, "May I?"

Explaining OHLC charts

"So, OHLC and candlestick charts are very similar to line charts. The only difference is that instead of using a point to denote the data value, these charts use small diagrams to show multiple data points. Let's start with an OHLC chart." Bob notices our confused looks. "Sorry, OHLC stands for Open, High, Low, Close. So, for each day on our x axis, we represent four prices for the stock. Also, for each day we have a figure that looks like this." Bob draws a line with branches sticking off on each side.

"So, for each day we have a vertical line. The top of the line shows the highest price the stock reached during the day; the bottom shows the lowest price. The two bars extending sideways are called ticks. The tick on the left side shows the opening price, and the tick on the right shows the closing price."

Explaining candlestick charts

"Does this make sense so far?", Bob asks. We nod and he continues. "Candlestick charts are modifications of OHLC charts. Here's an interesting trivia tidbit. Candlestick charts were created in Japan in the mid-1800s to help with the rice trade." He pauses and then turns to the whiteboard and begins drawing again.

"These charts also have a vertical line showing the high and low prices. However, instead of using ticks on each side to denote the opening and closing prices, they have a bar called the **body** overlaid on the line. The body extends from the opening price to the closing price."

"The parts of the line extending above and below the body are called the **shadows**. Sometimes, they are also called the **wick** and **tail**, hence the name **candlestick**. When the closing price is below the opening price, the body is filled in. If the closing price is higher than the opening price, the body is empty." Bob finishes his two diagrams as shown in the following figure:

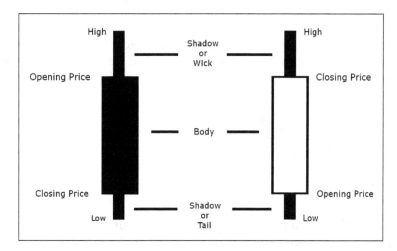

"This should be enough to get you going," Bob says as he sits down. Roshan continues the meeting, and the management team discusses other methods to improve enrollment. The meeting concludes after about an hour and we thank Bob as we leave.

Building an OHLC chart with last quarter's stock data

When we return to our office, we contact the IT team to get a JSON feed of the company's stock prices. They have one that was created a few months back. This gives us the stock prices of the last three quarters, which should be enough to get us started. We load the JSON feed in our browser and see that it is an array of arrays. For each array corresponding to a day, there are five elements: the date, the opening price, the high price, the low price, and the closing price:

```
[
["30-Sep-2012", 16.91, 17.29, 16.86, 17.16],
["29-Sep-2012", 16.70, 16.91, 16.46, 16.89],
...
]
```

With an understanding of the format of our remote data, we begin coding our chart using the following steps:

1. We start by including the OHLC plugin file. We also include the highlighter plugin so that we can show all the prices when the user highlights each day. In addition, we want the plugins that allow us to format our dates on the axis and rotate them:

```
<script src="../js/jqplot.ohlcRenderer.min.js"></script>
<script src="../js/jqplot.highlighter.min.js"></script>
<script src="../js/jqplot.dateAxisRenderer.min.js"></script>
<script src="../js/jqplot.canvasTextRenderer.min.js"></script>
<script src="../js/jqplot.canvasAxisTickRenderer.min.js"></script>
<script src="../js/functions.js"></script>
```

2. Since the JSON feed returns an array, we can reuse our `dataPull` function to wrap the `remoteData` array in another array:

```
<script>
$(document).ready(function(){
  function dataPull(remoteData,options) {
    return [remoteData];
  }
```

3. We set the title of our chart to the company's name and stock symbol. We also set the default angle and font size for our axis ticks:

```
var stockPrice = $.jqplot ('stockPrice', "./data/q1_q3_2012.
json",
  {
    title:'Q3 2012 - jQ Big Box Electronics (jqBBE)',
```

```
axesDefaults: {
    tickRenderer: $.jqplot.CanvasAxisTickRenderer ,
    tickOptions: {
      angle: -30,
      fontSize: '9pt'
    }
},
```

4. We set the options for `dataRenderer`, and then set the color for our line to black. This way it will show up more clearly. Under the `series` options, we pass in the OHLC renderer to `renderer` and increase the thickness of our line:

```
dataRenderer: remoteDataCallback,
dataRendererOptions: { dataCallback: dataPull },
seriesColors: ['#000'],
series: [
  {
    renderer:$.jqplot.OHLCRenderer,
    rendererOptions: { lineWidth: 2 }
  }
],
```

5. Next, we move on to the *x* axis. For our ticks, we want the date in the format of *Jan 1, 2012*, so we set `formatString` to `%b %e, %Y`:

```
axes:{
  xaxis:{
    renderer:$.jqplot.DateAxisRenderer,
    tickOptions: { formatString:'%b %e, %Y' },
```

6. Even though our JSON feed has 9 months of data, we can limit how much data appears on our chart using the `min` and `max` options. Since we are using `DateAxisRenderer`, we pass in a date and time instead of an integer or float:

```
max: "09-30-2012 16:00",
min: "07-01-2012 16:00"
},
```

7. Looking at the remote data, we notice the stock price stayed above 15. We make this the `min` value to reduce the empty space at the bottom of our chart. We also use the `prefix` option to prepend a dollar sign to our ticks. By default, jqPlot formats ticks as integers. Our prices use decimals, so we set `formatString` to `%.2f`, which formats our ticks as a float with two decimal places:

```
yaxis: {
  min: 15,
```

```
        label: 'Share Price',
        tickOptions: { prefix: '$', formatString: '%.2f' }
      }
    },
```

8. We use the highlighter plugin so that we can display all five array elements for each data point. We set `tooltipAxes` to `xy` so that our date will appear in our string, followed by the four `y` values. We then need to set the `yvalues` option to `4` so jqPlot will know that the three remaining elements are part of the *y* axis:

```
highlighter: {
    show: true,
    showMarker:false,
    tooltipLocation:'w',
    tooltipAxes: 'xy',
    yvalues: 4,
```

9. We finish the setup for our tooltip by setting `formatString`. We create a table with the date in the first row, and then we create a row for each price. We also use `%.2f` to format our prices as floats, with two decimal places like our ticks:

```
formatString:'<table class="jqplot-highlighter"> \
<tr><td colspan="2">Date: %s</td></tr> \
<tr><td>Open</td><td>%.2f</td> \
<tr><td>High</td><td>%.2f</td></tr> \
<tr><td>Low</td><td>%.2f</td></tr> \
<tr><td>Close</td><td>%.2f</td></tr> \
</table>'
      }
    });
  });
</script>
```

 Be aware, you can set your tooltip to display floating numbers, but if you do not format your axis ticks, then the values displayed in the tooltip will be rounded to the nearest whole number and will show zeroes for the decimal places.

10. We finish our chart by making the tooltip background opaque so that it is more legible when displayed. Since our tooltip is created inside a div element, we have the full use of CSS to style the tooltip:

```
<div id="stockPrice" style="width:600px;"></div>
<style>
.jqplot-highlighter-tooltip { background: rgba(208,208,208,1);}
.jqplot-highlighter td { padding-right: 5px; text-align: right;}
</style>
```

With all this complete, we save our work and load the chart in our browser. We hover over one of the lines and see our tooltip appear with all our data points:

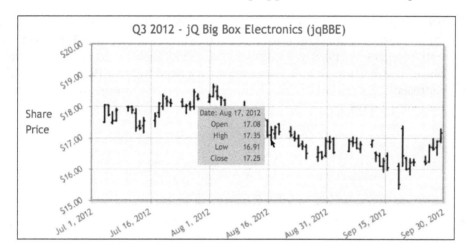

Building a candlestick chart with filtered data

We are happy with how our OHLC chart turned out. Now, we turn our attention to creating a candlestick chart. We consider this might work well on the dashboard.

We open the OHLC chart we just created and save it as a new file. We only need to set one option to make it a candlestick chart, but we also want to make a few other cosmetic changes. We execute the following steps:

1. The first change is the data feed that will pull in the stock prices of the last 14 days. We also update our title:

```
. . .
var stockPrice = $.jqplot ('stockPrice', "./data/last_14.json",
{
    title:'Last 14 Days - jQ Big Box Electronics (jqBBE)',
```

2. Under `rendererOptions` for our series, we set `candleStick` to `true`:

```
. . .
    series: [
      {
        renderer:$.jqplot.OHLCRenderer,
        rendererOptions: {
          lineWidth: 2,
          candleStick: true
        }
      }
    ],
```

3. Previously, we used `numberTicks` to limit the number of ticks jqPlot created for our axes. For this chart, we decide to use `tickInterval`. When dealing with integers, we pass in a number and jqPlot creates ticks at that interval. Since we are using `DateAxisRenderer`, we need to pass. We pass in a string representing a period of time. Since it is a short time frame, we set our ticks for every 2 days:

```
. . .
    xaxis:{
      renderer:$.jqplot.DateAxisRenderer,
      tickOptions: { formatString:'%b %e, %Y' },
      tickInterval: "2 days",
```

4. We also set the `max` and `min` options to our new time frame. We set the `min` option to 1 day before, so that our first candlestick is not cut off:

```
      max: "12-06-2012 16:00",
      min: "11-21-2012 00:00"
    },
```

5. We change the minimum value for our *y* axis to `20`.

```
    yaxis: {
      min: 20,
      label: 'Share Price',
      tickOptions: { prefix: '$', formatString: '%.2f' }
    }
  },
. . .
```

Now that we have completed our new candlestick chart, we load it in our browser. At a glance, we see that most days the stock closed higher than the opening price. We highlight the candlestick for November 28 and see our tooltip explaining what we see in the body of the candlestick. The stock opened at **21.75** and closed at **21.85**. We can tell on the next day that there was a big difference between the opening and closing prices, and the closing price was lower.

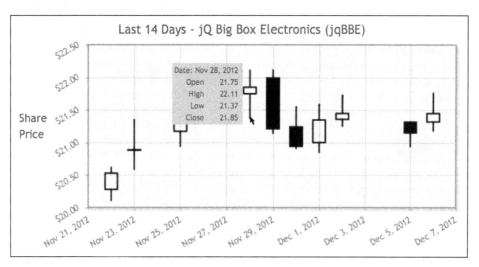

We decide now is a good time to go for lunch. As we get up to leave, Calvin and Bob stop by the office.

"I really like the candlestick charts," Calvin says. Bob points at the screen. He says, "One variation of a candlestick chart uses colors to signify whether a stock closes higher or not. If it closes higher, the body is colored green, and if it closes lower, the body is red. Some people color the body blue for a higher closing price, but I like red and green. It matches traffic lights and is intuitive."

Calvin interrupts, "Bob and I have a work lunch with some of the VPs. That reminds me, Roshan wanted to know if you can zoom in on the data in a chart. He specifically mentioned those charts where they cover a year or more of data." We mention that it is possible. "Cool. Why don't you generate a colored candlestick chart like Bob mentioned, with a year's worth of data? It will let you test out the zoom feature. Bob and I will swing by later this afternoon and see where you're at." We agree, and Calvin and Bob leave. We grab our things and head for lunch as well.

Zooming in on a colored candlestick chart

We get back from lunch and jump into creating the colored candlestick chart for Calvin. It will only require a couple of changes to our previous chart. We save the original as a new file, and then begin our modifications executing the following steps:

1. We include the cursor plugin file because the zooming feature is part of the cursor plugin:

    ```
    <script src="../js/jqplot.cursor.min.js"></script>
    <script>
    $(document).ready(function(){
      function dataPull(remoteData,options) {
        return [remoteData];
      }
    ```

2. We add the `enablePlugins` option before we create our chart. This way we don't have to enable each plugin individually. Next, we change the remote data feed back to the JSON feed with the first three quarters of data, and we also update our title:

    ```
    $.jqplot.config.enablePlugins = true;
    var stockPrice = $.jqplot ('stockPrice', "./data/q1_q3_2012.json",
      {
        title:'Q1-Q3 2012 - jQ Big Box Electronics (jqBBE)',
        axesDefaults: {
            tickRenderer: $.jqplot.CanvasAxisTickRenderer ,
            tickOptions: {
              angle: -30,
              fontSize: '9pt'
            }
        },
    ```

3. We add a few options to color our candlesticks. We start by setting `wickColor` to `#000`. If we don't, the wick and tail of each candlestick will render with the color of the body:

    ```
    . . .
        series: [
          {
            renderer:$.jqplot.OHLCRenderer,
            rendererOptions: {
              lineWidth: 2,
              candleStick:true,
              wickColor: '#000',
    ```

4. Next, we set `fillUpBody` to `true`. By default, this is `false`, so we want all candlestick bodies to be filled in. This brings us to the last two options to set, `upBodyColor` and `downBodyColor`. We set `upBodyColor` to the hexadecimal value of green and `downBodyColor` to the hexadecimal value of red:

```
        fillUpBody: true,
        upBodyColor: '#0f0',
        downBodyColor: '#f00'
      }
    }
  ],
```

5. For our *x* axis, we change our `min` and `max` values to match the upper and lower bounds of our JSON feed. We also decrease the `min` value for our *y* axis:

```
axes:{
  xaxis:{
    renderer:$.jqplot.DateAxisRenderer,
    tickOptions: { formatString:'%b %e, %Y' },
    max: "09-30-2012 16:00",
    min: "01-01-2012 16:00",
  },
  yaxis: {
    min: 12,
    label: 'Share Price',
    tickOptions: { prefix: '$', formatString: '%.2f' }
  }
},
```

6. To turn on the zooming function, we need to set the `cursor` option. We set `zoom` to `true`, and this will enable the zooming feature. We also turn off the tooltip by setting `showTooltip` to `false`:

```
cursor:{
  zoom: true,
  showTooltip: false
},
highlighter: {
  . . .
```

We load the new chart in our browser and notice a big change in price for one day in February:

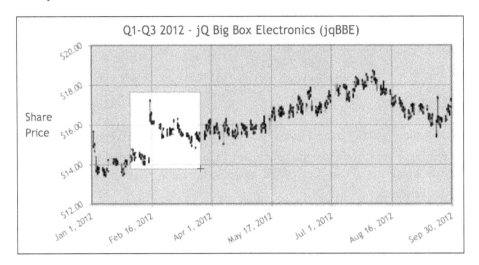

This is a good place to try out the zoom feature. We click on the chart and drag to draw a window around the area we want to zoom in on. The rest of the chart appears greyed out to make it easier for the user to see what they are zooming in on.

When we release the mouse button, the chart reloads to show the data we zoomed in on.

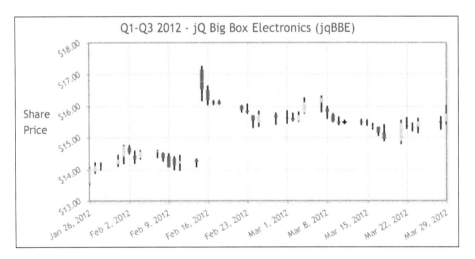

We also notice that the ticks for both the x and y axes are updated. When the price jumped on February 15, the price closed lower, and we know this because the body is red. When we are done, we double-click on the chart to reset to the original size.

Adding tooltips to canvas overlay lines

We wrap up our work and prepare for a little bit of relaxing reading on Reddit when Calvin, Bob, and Roshan stop by. We show Roshan the first two charts, and then show off our colored candlestick chart. Roshan asks, "Can we just make the bigger chart a line chart? I'm afraid all the extra marks and what not will confuse users." We tell him that won't be a problem.

We also point out the price jump on February 15. "Right," Roshan says, "that was the day the quarterly earnings were released. Actually, some of the numbers were leaked over the weekend, and the stock jumped before the market opened."

Roshan stops and looks like he is thinking something over. "You added a line to one of the bar charts, showing a threshold. Can you do something similar to denote when the quarterly earnings were released?" We tell him we should be able to do that. "Excellent. I look forward to seeing it. Now, we'll get out of your hair."

We save the previous chart as a new file and begin making our changes using the following steps:

1. To add canvas overlay lines, we include the corresponding plugin file. Since we are using three non-rendering plugins, we use `enablePlugins` to turn them all on. Then, we create the `canvasOverlay` option:

    ```
    . . .
    <script src="../js/jqplot.canvasOverlay.min.js"></script>
    . . .
      $.jqplot.config.enablePlugins = true;
      var stockPrice = $.jqplot ('stockPrice', "./data/q1_q3_2012.
    json", {
        . . .
        canvasOverlay: {
    ```

2. Next, we create the `objects` array. We set each of our three lines to `dashedVerticalLine`. For the first line, we set the name to `Q4 2011 Earnings`. With our previous lines, we set x to our threshold, which was an integer. Since we are using dates, we need to convert our date to a valid ISO 8601 timestamp so that jqPlot can place it properly:

    ```
    objects: [
      {
        dashedVerticalLine: {
          name: 'Q4 2011 Earnings',
          x: new Date("2012-02-15T06:00:00").getTime(),
    ```

3. Most of the other options are the same as before. However, this time we make use of the showTooltip option and set it to true. Then, we set tooltipLocation to e so that it will not overlap our highlighter tooltip. We finish by setting tooltipFormatString to the name of our line. We'll use the same layout for the other two lines, but change the x value, name, and tooltipFormatString:

```
                lineWidth: 2,
                color: '#00f',
                shadow: false,
                yOffset: 0,
                showTooltip: true,
                tooltipLocation:'e',
                tooltipFormatString: 'Q4 2011 Earnings'
            }
        },
        ...
    ]
},
...
```

4. We remove the renderer option from the series object. Then, we set showMarker to false, so we'll only show the line and not all the data points. We also set lineWidth to 1 so that the line is not so thick:

```
    series: [ { showMarker: false, lineWidth: 1 } ],
    ...
```

With all of that wrapped, we load the chart in our browser. We hover over the middle line, and the tooltip appears and shows **Q1 2012 Earnings**.

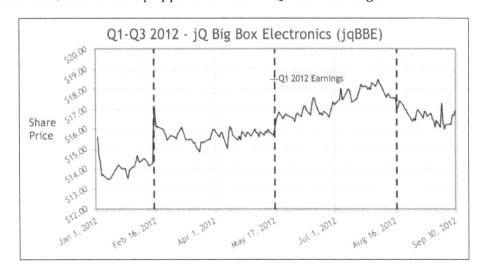

We zoom in to look at the month of July and notice something as we hover over the data point for July 6. The numbers in the tooltip don't seem to match the line.

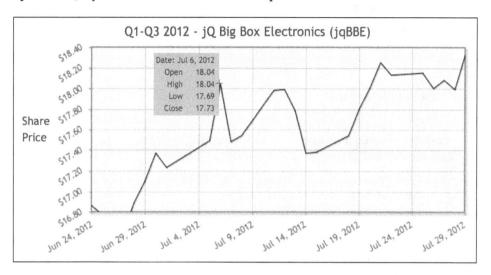

Our chart uses the opening price as the y value for our line, ignoring the other elements in the array. We need to swap the opening price with the closing price on the y axis, but we want to keep all the other values for the tooltip.

Modifying the data array and the tooltip

In order to remedy this problem, we need the closing price to be the first y value in our data array. We can accomplish this by modifying our dataPull function. We save the previous code as a new file and start making our changes executing the following steps:

1. We create a new array called stocks, and then loop through the remoteData array. We add the date, which is the first element, and then we add the closing price, which is the last element in the remoteData array:

   . . .
   ```
   function dataPull(remoteData,options) {
     var stocks = new Array;
     for(var x=0;x<remoteData.length;x++){
       stocks[x] = new Array;
       stocks[x].push(remoteData[x][0],remoteData[x][4]);
   ```

2. We now have our x and y values, so we loop through the rest of the prices in the child array. Once we finish working through `remoteData`, we return our new array to jqPlot:

```
for(var y=1;y<remoteData[x].length;y++){
    stocks[x].push(remoteData[x][y]);
  }
}
return [stocks];
}
```

3. Next, we change a few settings in the highlighter. We update `yvalues` to 5 to accommodate the new value in our data array:

```
. . .
    highlighter: {
      show: true,
      showMarker:false,
      tooltipLocation:'w',
      tooltipAxes: 'xy',
      yvalues: 5,
```

4. Before, we used CSS to hide a value in our tooltip. The other option is to use reordering. We use $ preceded by the value's position in the array, and place it between the % character and the rest of the formatting. Since the date is first in the array, we change it to `%1$s` instead of using `%s`. Next, we skip the first closing price, which is `%2$.2f`. Then, we format the four other prices:

```
    formatString:'<table class="jqplot-highlighter"> \
    <tr><td colspan="2">Date: %1$s</td></tr> \
    <tr><td>Open</td><td>%3$.2f</td> \
    <tr><td>High</td><td>%4$.2f</td></tr> \
    <tr><td>Low</td><td>%5$.2f</td></tr> \
    <tr><td>Close</td><td>%6$.2f</td></tr> \
    </table>'
  }
. . .
```

We reload our chart and zoom in on July 6. As we can see, our closing price was used to plot the line, and the correct prices match with the correct labels. We think Roshan will like this.

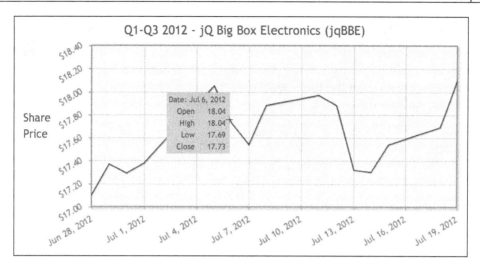

Close to 5 o'clock, Roshan and Calvin stop by. "We're on our way out and wanted to see what you came up with," Calvin says. We show Roshan the chart displaying the closing prices and the tooltips on the vertical lines. "That looks great. This is coming together more quickly than I thought. Now, go home and get some rest," Roshan says as he and Calvin turn to leave. We grab our things and follow behind them.

"Oh," Calvin says as he and Roshan walk out the door. "Sara wants to talk tomorrow about inventory and look at other chart types beyond what you already created."

Learning questions

1. What does OHLC stand for?

2. What are the different parts of a candlestick chart?

3. How can you skip over values in a tooltip using `formatString`?

4. Which plugin contains the zoom functionality?

5. Which options are needed to color the body of our candlesticks?

6. We added vertical lines to our chart to try to explain outside influences on the stock price. What other events might we visualize to help explain the changes in price?

7. What is the difference between the dates used for the x and y axes and the x or y values for a canvas overlay line?

8. What kind of data represented by different line charts can we add to a stock price chart to look for correlations?

Summary

We started this chapter by learning about OHLC and candlestick charts and their benefits over a simple line chart. We then went on to build both types of charts and learned how to limit the date range shown on our charts. We learned how to implement and use the zoom function.

Later, we created canvas overlay lines and added tooltips so that we could understand what each one was. We finished by learning how to skip over values passed into our tooltips. In the next chapter, we will look at when and how to use bubble charts, block plots, and waterfall charts.

8

Bubble Charts, Block Plots, and Waterfalls

So far, we've looked at line charts, bar charts, pie charts, and even charts used for the stock market. In this chapter, we will look at three other charts: the bubble chart and the block plot, which are similar to scatter plots, and the waterfall chart, which is a type of bar chart. In this chapter, we will:

- Discuss what a bubble chart is and the new data points we'll need to pass into our data arrays
- Create a bubble chart showing the revenue, units sold, and percentage of total profit
- Discuss how a block plot is similar to and different from a bubble chart
- Plot various product categories containing the revenue and units sold as data points
- Look at how waterfall charts visualize positive and negative data points

Creating a waterfall chart with expenses against revenue

The next morning, we come in and try and catch up on tasks that were put on hold when the dashboard project came around. Around 10 o'clock, Sara stops by. "Morning, you two. So, I have a few more requests for you."

Deciding on new chart types

"In my department, we have been looking at our vendors. We are trying to figure out which ones are not performing as well. If some are underperforming, we want to cut them. With the newly released funds, we can try and work out better deals with our existing, better performing vendors."

Sara continues, "I'll leave the implementation up to you, but I want to look at the revenue and units sold for the TV manufacturers we sell. If we can then expand this out into computers and DVD players as well, that would be great. These categories have the highest margins for us."

Sara pauses for a moment, "I hate to rush you, but I need these charts for a presentation later this week. Can you use something instead of a bar chart or line graph?" We assure her we will find a solution.

Sara stands to leave. "I'll get the numbers together and send them over this afternoon." I ask her if she can send over the profit numbers as well. She agrees and heads back to her office.

Understanding bubble charts

We sit down to begin discussing what kind of chart we can use for Sara's project. I mention this project would be a good use for a bubble chart because it will allow us to plot a third data point.

Bubble charts use three data points. The first two points are plotted on the x and y axes like a normal line chart. However, the third point is plotted as the size of the bubble. Some charts create the bubble using the third point as the radius of the bubble, and others use it as the area. These differences can affect how charts are interpreted. Also, the simple fact of having a user trying to determine which circle is larger can be difficult. So, along with the visualization of the data with bubbles, it is also recommended to label the elements to aid understanding. We can see an example in the following screenshot:

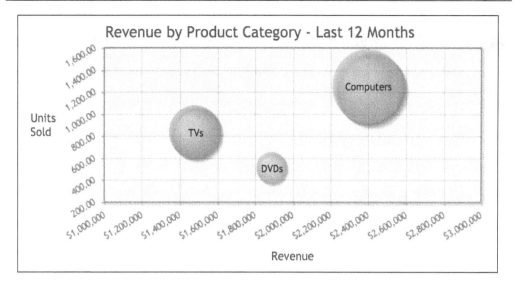

Since each data series is independent of each other, bubble charts are considered a part of the scatterplot family. So, with Sara's chart, we can plot the total revenue for each manufacturer on the x axis, and the total units sold on the y axis. For the bubble size, we can pass in the percentage of profit generated by the manufacturer. This will give Sara a good indication of which manufacturers are performing well and which have the higher margins.

Building a bubble chart

We finish our planning and decide to grab lunch since we're still waiting on data from Sara. When we return to the office, we have an e-mail waiting for us from Sara with the manufacturer revenue numbers she promised us this morning:

1. We begin coding our chart by including the `bubbleRenderer` plugin file along with the highlighter and canvas plugin files:

    ```
    <script src="../js/jqplot.bubbleRenderer.min.js"></script>
    <script src="../js/jqplot.highlighter.min.js"></script>
    <script src="../js/jqplot.canvasTextRenderer.min.js"></script>
    <script src="../js/jqplot.canvasAxisTickRenderer.min.js"></script>
    <script src="../js/functions.js"></script>
    ```

2. Next, we create our data array. We place the total revenue in the first element for each data array followed by the units sold. Based on the numbers Sara sent us, we calculate the percentage of profit for each manufacturer and make this the third element. For the fourth element, we can pass in a label as a string or an object with a label and/or a color for the bubble:

```
<script>
$(document).ready(function(){
 var tv_manufacturers =
   [
     [148474, 226, 20.22, "Kogan"],
     [166778, 261, 14.87, "Beko"],
     [139054, 205, 12.24, "Akurra"],
     [88143,  118, 8.79, "Finlux"],
     [179734, 316, 15.93, "Vestel"],
     [280141, 446, 27.95, "Sansui"]
   ];
```

3. We move on to create the plot and set `title` and `axesDefaults`:

```
var bubbleChart = $.jqplot ('bubbleChart', [tv_manufacturers],
{
    title:'Revenue in TV Category by Manufacturer - Last 12
Months',
    axesDefaults: {
        tickRenderer: $.jqplot.CanvasAxisTickRenderer ,
        tickOptions: {
          angle: -30,
          fontSize: '9pt'
        }
    },
```

4. We format the *x* axis to display the revenue with a dollar sign and thousand place separators. For the *y* axis, we format the values to two decimal places. We don't need this for the actual *y* axis, but because we want our percent of profit to show two decimal places, we need to set this option. This is because jqPlot considers the third element a *y* axis value:

```
axes:{
  xaxis:{
    label: 'Revenue',
    tickOptions: { formatString: "$%'d" }
  },
  yaxis: {
    label: 'Units Sold',
    tickOptions: { formatString: "%'.2f" }
  }
},
```

5. We make use of the highlighter plugin to show all the values for each data series. We set `tooltipOffset` to 5 so that our tooltip will not crowd the label of each bubble. Since we want to use actual percentage signs in `formatString`, we need to use two percentage signs. This way, the second percentage sign will be treated as a character:

```
highlighter: {
  show: true,
  tooltipOffset: 5,
  yvalues: 2,
  formatString:"<table border='0'> \
  <tr><td>Revenue:</td><td class='right'>%s</td></tr> \
  <tr><td>Units Sold:</td><td class='right'>%d</td></tr> \
  <tr><td>%% of Profit:</td><td class='right'>%.2f%%</td><//
tr></table>"
  },
```

6. Under `seriesDefaults`, we set `renderer` to `$.jqplot.BubbleRenderer`. Bubble charts allow for a gradient on the bubble, so we set `bubbleGradients` to `true`. Since some of our bubbles might cover the rest, we set `bubbleAlpha` to `0.6` so that we can see through the bubbles. We also set `highlightAlpha` to `0.8` so that when we highlight a bubble, it becomes less translucent, and it's easier to see the label and full size of the bubble. We also make the bubbles stand out more by setting `shadow` to `true`:

```
seriesDefaults:{
  renderer: $.jqplot.BubbleRenderer,
  rendererOptions: {
    bubbleGradients: true,
    bubbleAlpha: 0.6,
    highlightAlpha: 0.8,
  },
  shadow: true
  }
  });
});
</script>
```

7. We finish our chart by creating the div to contain the plot and add some CSS to format the tooltip. We set `z-index` to 99 so that the tooltip will always appear on top of the bubble. We also set the background to be opaque so that the tooltip will be easier to read:

```
<div id="bubbleChart" style="width:600px;"></div>
<style>
.jqplot-highlighter-tooltip { background: rgba(208,208,208,1);
z-index: 99; padding: 5px;}
.jqplot-highlighter td { padding-right: 5px; text-align: right;}
</style>
```

We save our work, and then preview the results in a browser, which are shown in the following screenshot:

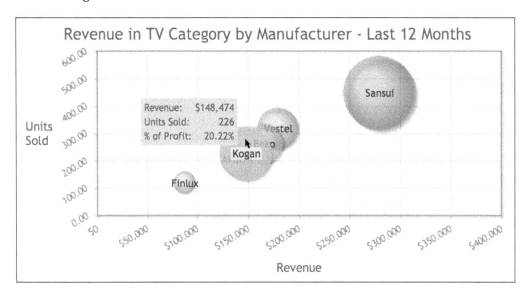

The bubbles have a nice gradient fill. They are also in a line, and this suggests a trend: the more units sold, the more revenue generated. Since we expected this outcome, it won't be necessary to include a trend line. We hover our mouse over the group of bubbles in the middle and highlight **Kogan**.

Based on the size of the bubble and the text in the tooltip, we see that Kogan TVs accounted for 20 percent of our profits, but we sold less units than some of the neighboring manufacturers. So, we can say that the profit margin for Kogan TV is higher than Beko or Vestel. This will be useful to Sara.

Building a block plot

We receive another e-mail from Sara. She forgot to send us numbers for the other electronics categories she wanted us to chart. Having created a bubble chart, we decide to create a block plot.

A block plot is one of those charts that has different implementations or definitions. Block plots in jqPlot are similar to bubble charts, but the data points are rendered as a block instead of as a bubble. Also, block plots only use x and y values, so the blocks are all of the same size. Their sizes will differ slightly because of the length of the label for each data point. An example of a block plot can be seen in the following screenshot:

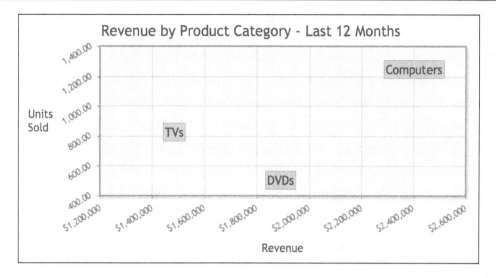

After looking at the data from Sara's e-mail, there will be 17 data points on our chart. It is likely that some blocks will overlap others, and it may be hard to see some of the blocks. We will use the enhanced legend plugin, which will give us the ability to hide certain data series. So, for example, we can hide the **TVs** and **Computers** categories and only show the **DVDs** category:

1. To get started, we include the `blockRenderer` plugin file along with the `highlighter`, `enhancedLegendRenderer`, and `canvasTextRenderer` plugin files:

```
<script src="../js/jqplot.blockRenderer.min.js"></script>
<script src="../js/jqplot.highlighter.min.js"></script>
<script src="../js/jqplot.enhancedLegendRenderer.min.js"></script>
<script src="../js/jqplot.canvasTextRenderer.min.js"></script>
<script src="../js/jqplot.canvasAxisTickRenderer.min.js"></script>
<script src="../js/functions.js"></script>
<script>
$(document).ready(function(){
```

2. Next, we include arrays with the values for TV, computer, and DVD player manufacturers:

```
var tv_manufacturers =
    [
    [226, 148474, "Kogan"],
    [261, 166778, "Beko"],
    [205, 139054, "Akurra"],
    [118, 88143,  "Finlux"],
    [316, 179734, "Vestel"],
```

```
      [446, 280141, "Sansui"]
      ];

   var computer_manufacturers =
      [
        [325, 238978, "Konvex"],
        [367, 310553, "Luxor"],
        [226, 170127, "Sperry"],
        [121, 87008, "Finlux"],
        [259, 180924, "Hasee"],
        [295, 251509, "Olidata"],
        [497, 405308, "Akurra"]
      ];

   var dvd_player_manufacturers =
      [
        [248, 61147, "BenQ"],
        [255, 51107, "Cinram"],
        [100, 14695, "Finlux"],
        [334, 72634, "Akurra"],
      ];
```

3. Now, we create the variable to hold our jqPlot object and pass in the three data arrays. We set the `title` and `axesDefaults` values:

```
var blockPlot = $.jqplot ('blockPlot', [tv_manufacturers,
computer_manufacturers, dvd_player_manufacturers],
   {
     title:'Revenue for Various Categories by Manufacturer',
     axesDefaults: {
         tickRenderer: $.jqplot.CanvasAxisTickRenderer ,
         tickOptions: {
           angle: -30,
           fontSize: '9pt'
         }
     },
```

4. For this chart, we decide to swap the axes, putting **Revenue** on the *y* axis and **Units Sold** on the *x* axis. Since we are not passing in floating values, we set both `formatString` options to $%'d:

```
axes:{
  yaxis:{
    label: 'Revenue',
    min: 0,
    tickOptions: { formatString: "$%'d" }
```

```
  },
  xaxis: {
    label: 'Units Sold',
    tickOptions: { formatString: "%'d" }
  }
},
```

5. The only new option for the legend is to set `renderer` to `EnhancedLegendRenderer`:

```
legend:{
  renderer: $.jqplot.EnhancedLegendRenderer,
  show:true,
  placement: 'outsideGrid'
},
```

6. For `seriesDefaults`, we set `renderer` to `BlockRenderer`, and we enable `shadows` to make the chart more visually appealing:

```
seriesDefaults:{
  renderer: $.jqplot.BlockRenderer,
  shadow: true
},
```

7. We want custom colors for each data series, and we want to lower the opacity, so we set the color using the `rgba` format. With translucent blocks, users will be able to see through them if they overlap:

```
series: [
  { label: 'TVs', color: 'rgba(255, 150, 12, .6)' },
  { label: 'Computers', color: 'rgba(160, 160, 255, .6)' },
  { label: 'DVD Players', color: 'rgba(86, 194, 174, .6)' },
],
```

8. We use the same configuration for our block plot that we used for our bubble chart. Since the background of our blocks is translucent, it is possible to see the data point that jqPlot renders underneath the block. So, we add the `showMarker` option and set it to `false`. Since we are only passing in the block label behind the *y* axis value, we set `yvalues` to 2:

```
highlighter: {
  show: true,
  showMarker: false,
  tooltipOffset: 5,
  yvalues: 2,
  formatString:"<table border='0'><tr><td colspan='2'
align='center'>%3$s</td></tr> \
    <tr><td>Units Sold:</td><td class='right'>%1$d</td></tr> \
```

```
        <tr><td>Revenue:</td><td class='right'>%2$s</td></tr></
table>"
      }
    });
  });
</script>
```

9. We finish by adding the div to contain our plot and the CSS we created for our bubble chart. It will be useful for this chart as well:

```
<div id="blockPlot" style="width:600px;"></div>
<style>
.jqplot-highlighter-tooltip { background: rgba(208,208,208,1);
z-index: 99;}
.jqplot-highlighter td { padding-right: 5px; text-align: right;}
</style>
```

We load the chart and hover over the block for **Hasee** under **Computers**. We can see what the chart looks like in the following screenshot. The chart looks good, but as we thought, many of the blocks overlap.

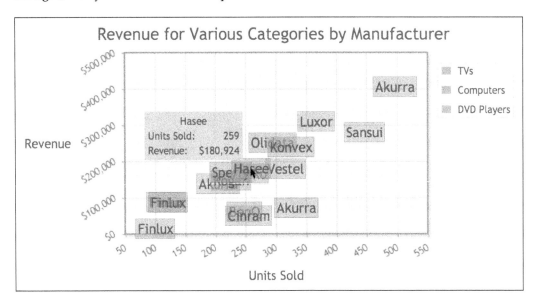

We want to see only the **Computers** category, so we click on the **TVs** category in the legend first. We see that jqPlot draws a line through the legend item and all the **TVs** blocks fade out. Next, we click on the **DVDs** category; the blocks fade out and the legend item is also crossed out. We are now left with only the **Computers** category.

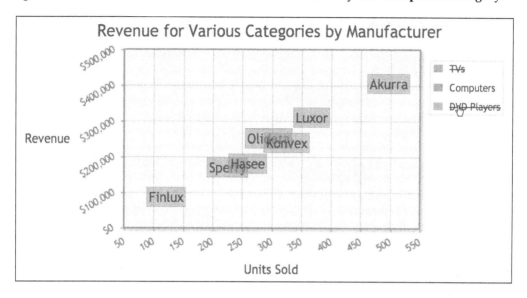

As we wrap up for the day, Calvin stops by and we show him the two charts we created for Sara. "I like them. They're different from bar charts, and you can still get to all the relevant data with the tooltips and what not."

Calvin continues, "Roshan wants a quick meeting in the morning with you two. I'll have Sara sit in, and we can show her the charts you did today. Well, I'll see you tomorrow morning." He turns and leaves. We grab our things and follow behind him.

Gaining our next set of requirements

The next morning we meet with Calvin, Roshan, and Sara in a small conference room. We walk Sara through the charts and she loves them. "These will be perfect for my presentation."

Then, Roshan speaks up, "And now for my request. I was telling Calvin I have been reading this great book called *The McKinsey Way, Ethan Rasiel, McGraw-Hill*. It had a great section on charting data. One chart mentioned a waterfall chart." I hold up my hand, "We have never heard of a waterfall chart. What does it do?"

Roshan continues, "It shows how certain data points impact others. It looks like a bar chart, but some of the bars are floating. I'm not explaining it well. I'm sure you can find more information about them. I want a waterfall chart showing revenue along with operating expenses and fixed costs."

Sara gets a quizzical look on her face. "Are inventory losses included in your operating expenses?" Roshan stops to think. "No, they're not." Sara continues, "In that case, I would like to add inventory losses as an item to the chart."

I speak up, "Roshan, if you and Sara compile the numbers for us, we'll look at creating one for you." Roshan nods, "That sounds good. I'd like to see this chart by Friday. I've got a presentation with the rest of the VPs."

Understanding waterfall charts

We head back to our office and start our research. We spend about an hour and finally get a grasp on how waterfall charts work. Waterfall charts show how our starting value is affected by other data values. Once all the effects are plotted, we are left with our final value.

We are looking at how various expenses affect revenue. So, once all the expenses are deducted, we are left with our profit. So, revenue will be our starting value and profit will be the final value.

Our starting and final values will be full bars extending from zero upward on the y axis. Each of the values in between will begin at the y value of the previous bar. If the value is positive, the new bar will extend up, and the bar will extend down if the value is negative. Generally, the bars are color-coded to easily show which values are negative and which are positive.

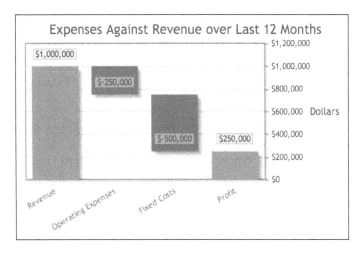

Let's say our revenue is $1,000,000. The next value is operating expenses which totals to $250,000. The bar for operating expenses will start at $1,000,000, extend downward, and stop at $750,000. Fixed costs stand at $500,000. So, the bar will start at $750,000 and extend down to $250,000. The last bar is profit, and it will be calculated based on the other numbers. It is a positive number, so it will extend from $0 to $250,000. It's easy to see how the chart got its name. Each value moves downward like a waterfall.

Creating a waterfall chart showing expenses against revenue

While we were completing our research, Roshan and Sara sent us the numbers. With everything we need, we get started executing the following steps:

1. To make a waterfall chart, we need to include the `barRenderer` plugin file. Tooltips do not work with negative values on waterfall charts, so we include the `pointLabels` plugin file, and we also add the `categoryAxisRenderer` plugin file:

```
<script src="../js/jqplot.barRenderer.min.js"></script>
<script src="../js/jqplot.pointLabels.min.js"></script>
<script src="../js/jqplot.categoryAxisRenderer.min.js"></script>
<script src="../js/jqplot.canvasTextRenderer.min.js"></script>
<script src="../js/jqplot.canvasAxisTickRenderer.min.js"></script>
<script src="../js/functions.js"></script>
<script>
```

2. We include Roshan's numbers for revenue and expenses and Sara's returns number. Roshan sent over a profit number, but jqPlot will calculate that number automatically, so we won't include it in our data arrays. Since the other three numbers are expenses, we'll need to set them to negative numbers so that our waterfall is calculated properly:

```
$(document).ready(function(){
  var revenue = 9631203;
  var operating_expenses = -3497514;
  var fixed_costs = -3036541;
  var returns = -802798;
```

3. Next, we create our plot and pass in the data arrays. We set the renderer to BarRenderer, and then we set the waterfall option under rendererOptions to true to make our chart a waterfall. We set useNegativeColors to true; this will color all positive values with one color and all negative values with another. Finally, we set highlightMouseOver to false. Negative value bars do not have the highlight ability, so we'll turn them off for the positive values so as not to confuse the user:

```
var waterFall = $.jqplot ('waterFall', [[revenue, operating_
expenses, fixed_costs, returns]],
  {
    title:'Expenses Against Revenue over Last 12 Months',
    seriesDefaults:{
      renderer:$.jqplot.BarRenderer,
      rendererOptions:{
        waterfall:true,
        useNegativeColors: true,
        highlightMouseOver: false
      },
```

If we were not concerned with using colors to show negative and positive numbers, we could use varyBarColor. By setting this to true, each bar will be colored differently, and this will show that each value is independent.

4. Since we do not have the highlight option, we will make use of pointLabels. We set location to n, so the labels will appear above the y value for each bar. Also, we don't want the labels covering some of our smaller bars, so we set ypadding to 10. This will move the labels further toward the top of the chart. Also, we set yaxis to y2axis, so the ticks and labels will appear on the right side of the chart:

```
    pointLabels:{ show:true, location:'n', ypadding:10 },
    yaxis:'y2axis'
  },
```

5. For our *y* axis, we add our label and format the ticks to display the currency in dollars:

```
axes:{
  y2axis:{
    label: 'Dollars',
    tickOptions: { formatString: "$%'d" }
  },
```

6. For our *x* axis, we set `renderer` to `CategoryAxisRenderer`. We also set ticks to an array of our values. We have five ticks, but we only pass in four data arrays. This is because jqPlot will calculate the **Profit** bar for us automatically. We also turn off the gridlines and tick marks by setting `showGridline` and `showMark` under `tickOptions` to `false`:

```
xaxis:{
    renderer:$.jqplot.CategoryAxisRenderer,
    ticks: ['Revenue', 'Operating Expenses', 'Fixed Costs',
'Inventory Losses', 'Profit'],
    tickRenderer: $.jqplot.CanvasAxisTickRenderer,
    tickOptions: {
      angle: -30,
      fontSize: '9pt',
      showGridline: false,
      showMark: false
    }
  },
 },
});
});
</script>
```

7. We finish our chart by including the div container for our plot and adding some CSS to add a background and a border to our point labels:

```
<div id="waterFall" style="width:500px;height:400px;"></div>
<style>
.jqplot-point-label { background: rgba(208,208,208,.6); border:
1px solid #999; padding:0px 3px;}
</style>
```

Once we are done, we load the chart in our browser and can see the results:

The chart shows our starting value representing **Revenue**, and it then subtracts each expense, bringing us to our **Profit** value. We're pretty sure Roshan and Sara will like this. We e-mail Calvin to see if he can plan a meeting for some time this afternoon. With that done, we head to lunch.

When we get back from lunch, we find an e-mail from Calvin. We have a meeting scheduled in 30 minutes. We prepare everything for our presentation and head down to the conference room. We show Sara and Roshan the waterfall chart, and they love it. "I didn't realize our inventory losses were that high," says Roshan. "That is the exact reaction I'm going for," says Sara. "I want to get our inventory issues out there so we can figure out ways to fix them," she continues.

Roshan speaks up again, "After my meeting tomorrow, I think we'll be in a better place to know what the team wants on the dashboard. Then, we can start compiling all these different experiments into a coherent format ready to go into production."

We leave the meeting and head back to our office. We start to compile a list of possible API feeds we'll need in order to make our charts real time. We can check this list against the finalized charts from Roshan's meeting and contact IT with our requests later.

Learning questions

1. What option will we use to change the colors on our waterfall chart?

2. What are the other values, besides the x and y values, passed into a bubble chart?

3. We passed in a percentage as a float in our bubble chart. What option do we need to set in order for this value to be displayed as a float?

4. Bubble charts and block plots are similar to what other chart?

5. What plugin did we use to turn off the series in our block plot?

6. What other data sets might work well with a waterfall chart?

Summary

We started the chapter looking at how to create a bubble chart. This allowed us to plot a third data point beyond our x and y values. We then created a bubble chart showing different TV manufacturers with the revenue, units sold, and percentage of total profit for each.

Next, we discussed how to build a block plot, and then we plotted the revenue and units sold for each manufacturer in various product categories. We learned how to use the enhanced legend to remove data series in order to help us when looking at these series individually. Finally, we learned how to create a waterfall chart and plotted revenue and various company expenses.

In the next chapter, we will learn the `replot` and `redraw` methods. These methods will allow us to refresh our charts without reloading our web page. This will allow our charts to display real-time data.

9
Showing Real-time Data with Our Charts

Up to this point, most of our charts used static data stored within our HTML files. We made some interactive charts where we reloaded the data, but we had to reload the entire page. There are two methods in jqPlot: `redraw` and `replot`. These methods allow us to rebuild our charts without reloading the page.

In this chapter, we will cover the following topics:

- Creating a meter gauge chart showing current Wi-Fi users for a particular store
- Using the `replot` method to refresh the number of Wi-Fi users at set intervals
- Using the `replot` method to change the dataset our chart is using and update the chart accordingly
- Using `replot` to dynamically build our chart, based on the data received from the remote data source

We come to work on Friday morning and find Jeff from IT waiting for us. "Morning", he says. We ask him what we can do for him.

"I was talking with Sara yesterday," Jeff says. "She told me she was concerned about people coming into our store, browsing, and then going online to buy the same item. She asked if there was any way for us to know if people were looking at a competitor's site while in our stores."

Jeff continued, "So, I went back to my office and looked through our Wi-Fi access logs. Just over 50 percent of guest traffic is to competitor sites. This got me thinking. What if we sent sales messages to people's phones when they first got online in-store or just made an announcement over the PA system?"

I stop Jeff. "That's all feasible, but where do we come in?" Jeff nods, "Right, I was wondering if you can make some kind of chart or widget showing how many people are on the Wi-Fi network at a given time, and then update the information every few minutes?"

We look at each other. I answer Jeff, "If we can get access to the data from the Wi-Fi access points, then I think we can. Your department will have to create an API end point for us to connect to though."

Jeff nods again, "I'll get some of my guys on it. Can you make some kind of prototype with fake data to show Roshan, and then we can work in the real data later?" We assure him we can. Jeff stands to leave. "I really appreciate it. I'll check in with you later."

Creating a meter gauge chart with Wi-Fi users

We begin to ponder what kind of chart to use for Jeff's idea. After looking through the documentation, we decide to use jqPlot's meter gauge. It's a chart that resembles a gauge on a car dashboard, with a needle pointing to the given data point on the semicircular gauge.

We create a new HTML file and set about creating our meter gauge as follows:

1. We start by including the `MeterGaugeRenderer` plugin file. Since this is a prototype, we'll start by passing in a single value to the data array:

```
<script src="../js/jqplot.meterGaugeRenderer.min.js"></script>
<script>
$(document).ready(function(){
  var meter = $.jqplot('wifi', [[100]],
    {
```

2. We move on to `seriesDefaults` and start by setting the renderer to `$.jqplot.MeterGaugeRenderer`. After that, we begin setting some of the `rendererOptions` by setting the minimum and maximum values, as follows:

```
    seriesDefaults: {
      renderer: $.jqplot.MeterGaugeRenderer,
      rendererOptions: {
        min: 0,
        max: 255,
```

3. We also set label to `WIFI` users, and then set `ticks` at intervals of 50 using an array, as follows:

```
label: 'WIFI users',
ticks:[0, 50, 100, 150, 200, 250],
```

4. We want to make use of the `intervals` option. Assuming that Jeff will want to send messages when there are a certain number of people in the store, we set the intervals at 30, 175, 225, and 255. Each value will be the upper bound for the interval. This can be implemented as follows:

```
intervals:[30, 175, 225, 255],
```

5. Next, we override the default color scheme for our intervals and use the typical green, yellow, and red scheme. For our first interval, we don't want any color to appear, so we use the same color as the chart itself. Once the needle goes above 175, the interval will appear yellow, and anything above 225 will be red. The code for this is as follows:

```
intervalColors:['#efefef', '#66cc66', '#E7E658', '#f00']
        }
      }
    });
```

6. To make our chart update at set intervals, we will use `window.setInterval`, which is a standard JavaScript method. Since this is a prototype, we create a random number between 30 and 255:

```
window.setInterval(function() {
  var rnd = Math.floor(Math.random() * (255 - 30 + 1)) +
     30;
```

7. Next, we locate the element in the data series array located within our jqPlot object. We manually set this to 100 when we create the object. Now, we update it with a new array. Since we are only passing in one data point, we set the x value to `1` and then pass in `rnd` as the y value. Then, we call the `redraw` function, which will redraw the chart. We set the time interval to `5000`, so our chart will update every 5 seconds, as follows:

```
    meter.series[0].data[0] = [1,rnd];
    meter.redraw();
  }, 5000);
});
</script>
<div id="wifi" style="width:300px;height:200px;"></div>
<style>
.jqplot-meterGauge-label { font-size: 12px;}
</style>
```

We load the chart in our browser and see the following figure:

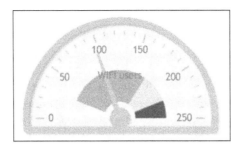

We see our gauge with the needle at 100. We also see the 4 intervals. The first interval appears blank because we set it to have the same color as the gauge. The green interval is large and is followed by the yellow and red intervals. The only downside is that our label appears in the middle of the gauge. If we were not using the colors, we would be able to read the label.

Then, we notice the chart is redrawn and the needle now appears near 200, as shown in the following figure:

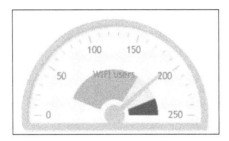

This is a good start. We decide to wait for Jeff's response before moving forward, so we move on to some smaller projects that have been waiting.

Refreshing our chart from remote data

About an hour later, Jeff stops back by the office. We show him our prototype. "This is cool. My guys are still trying to figure out how to pass the information from the routers to our web servers. In the meantime, I had them create a mock endpoint that you can test against. I told them to e-mail you the link." Jeff leaves, and a few minutes later, we receive an e-mail from Mark in IT.

We load the URL and see that the page contains the single array **[200]**. With this endpoint, we'll only need to change a few things in our meter.

We save our previous gauge chart as a new file and begin making our modifications, as follows:

1. We start by adding `dataPull` to format our data. We only need to wrap `remoteData` in an array, as shown in the following code snippet:

```
$(document).ready(function(){

  function dataPull(remoteData,options) {
    return [remoteData];
  }
```

> If your chart does not load the new data, you will need to set `cache` to `false` inside the AJAX method in our `remoteDataCallback` method located in `functions.js`.

2. Next, we pass in the JSON URL to our chart. Then, we set `remoteDataCallback` as our `dataRenderer`, which is the method that retrieves our remote data. After this, we set `dataPull` as our callback under `dataRendererOptions`:

```
var meter = $.jqplot('wifi', './data/wifi_users.json',
  {
    dataRenderer: remoteDataCallback,
    dataRendererOptions: { dataCallback: dataPull },
    seriesDefaults: {
      renderer: $.jqplot.MeterGaugeRenderer,
```

3. We don't want our label in the middle of our gauge, so we set `labelPosition` to `bottom`. Now, it will appear below our chart. This can be implemented by using the following code snippet:

```
rendererOptions: {
  min: 0,
  max: 255,
  label: 'WIFI users',
  labelPosition: 'bottom',
```

4. Since we want to refresh the data from a remote source, we need to use `replot` instead of `redraw`. We will also need to use `replot` if we want to change our ticks or axes. We set the `data` object to our JSON URL located on the server we are working on. When `setInterval` fires, it will pull the data again, and it will then replot all the data and axes:

```
window.setInterval(function() {
  meter.replot({ data: './data/wifi_users.json'});
}, 5000);
```

```
});
</script>
<div id="wifi" style="width:400px;"></div>
```

We load our updated chart, and everything looks like before, except that our label is below the gauge now, as shown in the following figure:

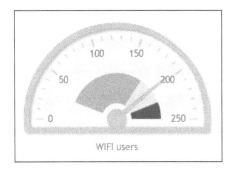

After 5 seconds, nothing changes. This is because the JSON Jeff created for us is currently static. If we look at our console though, we will see network traffic as a result of our script pulling the remote data. Once IT changes the endpoint to reflect dynamic data, our chart will begin to change.

Using the replot method to change remote datasets

We decide to grab an early lunch. When we get back, we start thinking about some of our other charts we could use the `replot` method on. Our stock chart that shows the last quarter's prices comes to mind. We contact IT, and they inform us they already have a couple of URLs to get the last 3, 6, 12, or 24 months of data. That's all we need. With the data sets we need, we can begin work:

1. We pull up the code for the stock chart and save it as a new file. We leave all the plugins from before:

```
<script src="../js/jqplot.ohlcRenderer.min.js"></script>
<script src="../js/jqplot.highlighter.min.js"></script>
<script
  src="../js/jqplot.dateAxisRenderer.min.js"></script>
<script
  src="../js/jqplot.canvasTextRenderer.min.js"></script>
<script
  src="../js/jqplot.canvasAxisTickRenderer.min.js"></script>
<script src="../js/functions.js"></script>
```

2. We add `dataPull` to take the data, and wrap it in an array for jqPlot. We also create a variable to hold part of our title:

```
<script>
$(document).ready(function(){
  function dataPull(remoteData,options) {
    return [remoteData];
  }
  var title = ' - jQ Big Box Electronics (jqBBE)';
```

3. When we first load the chart, we pull in the data of the last 3 months. If a user wants a different time frame, they can select it from the drop-down menu after the page loads. For the `title` option, we concatenate the `Past 3 Months` string and the `title` variable. We'll do the same with our other datasets later, and it will allow us to update the title of our chart:

```
$.jqplot.config.enablePlugins = true;
var stockPrice = $.jqplot ('stockPrice',
  "./data/3_months.json",
{
  title:'Past 3 Months'+title,
  axesDefaults: {
    tickRenderer: $.jqplot.CanvasAxisTickRenderer ,
    tickOptions: { angle: -30, fontSize: '9pt' }
  },
```

4. We include the `dataRenderer` option, and set `dataPull` as the callback for the `renderer` options:

```
dataRenderer: remoteDataCallback,
dataRendererOptions: { dataCallback: dataPull },
seriesColors: ['#000'],
series: [ { renderer:$.jqplot.OHLCRenderer } ],
```

5. We set the renderer for the *x* axis to use `DateAxisRenderer`, and we set the *y* axis to use a 2 decimal point float:

```
axes:{
  xaxis:{
    renderer:$.jqplot.DateAxisRenderer,
    tickOptions: { formatString:'%b %e, %Y' }
  },
  yaxis: {
    label: 'Share Price',
    tickOptions: { prefix: '$', formatString: '%.2f' }
  }
},
```

6. We are still using the highlighter, so we set `yvalues` to 4 and add the relevant markup to generate our tooltip:

```
highlighter: {
  showMarker:false,
  tooltipLocation:'w',
  tooltipAxes: 'xy',
  yvalues: 4,
  formatString:'<table class="jqplot-highlighter"> \
  <tr><td colspan="2">Date: %s</td></tr> \
  <tr><td>Open</td><td>%.2f</td> \
  <tr><td>High</td><td>%.2f</td></tr> \
  <tr><td>Low</td><td>%.2f</td></tr> \
  <tr><td>Close</td><td>%.2f</td></tr> \
  </table>'
  }
});
```

7. Next, we need an event handler for the select input we are going to create. Based on the selected value, we use this to create the URL for our JSON file. We will also update the title of our chart with the selected value, as follows:

```
$("#timeframe").change(function() {
  stockPrice.replot({
    data: './data/'+$(this).val()+'_months.json',
    title:'Past '+$(this).val()+' Months'+title
  });
});

});
</script>
```

8. Next, we add the `select` input above the div containing our chart:

```
<select id="timeframe" name="timeframe">
  <option value='3'>3 months</option>
  <option value='6'>6 months</option>
  <option value='12'>12 months</option>
  <option value='24'>24 months</option>
</select>
<div id="stockPrice" style="width:600px;"></div>
<style>
.jqplot-highlighter-tooltip { background:
  rgba(208,208,208,1);}
.jqplot-highlighter td { padding-right: 5px; text-align:
  right;}
</style>
```

We open the chart in our browser, and we can see that it has loaded the last 3 months of data, as shown in the following screenshot:

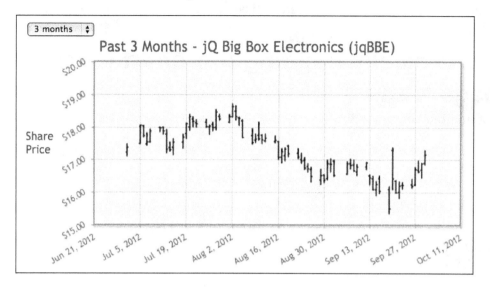

We select **24 months** from the drop-down menu, and the chart reloads without refreshing the page. We now see the stock prices of the last 2 years. We switch between the different time periods, and see that both the *x* and *y* axes change each time, as shown in the following screenshot:

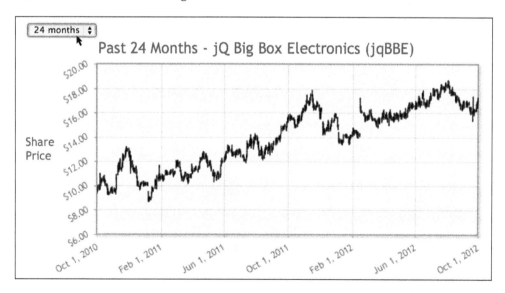

The ability to change the data feeds and refresh our charts without reloading the page opens up a lot of possibilities. We can build labels, ticks, and other elements from the remote data. This way there will be less static elements in our charts.

Dynamically building our chart when the page loads

We start thinking about the bar chart we made that showed various product categories and a trend line for a chosen category. We send off another e-mail to IT to see whether they can compile the data into a JSON feed. A few minutes later, we get a reply stating that Roshan has asked for the same thing. They are still trying to get everything working, but in the interim, they created a mock JSON feed. They also sent along the URL.

We load the JSON feed in our browser. They moved all the category data into an object called `categories`. They also created an object called `labels` to hold the ticks for our chart:

```
{
  "categories": {
    "TVs": [378583.39, 346552.99, 368164.98, 371856.60, 366457.82,
      327396.58],
    "Computers": [563621.35, 540214.96, 589978.66, 637114.31,
      621279.49, 599837.31],
    "DVDs/Blu-ray": [546643.33, 517902.14, 482774.32, 455892.62,
      438679.00, 406907.18],
    "Music CDs": [398583.39, 386552.99, 372738.46, 359209.91,
      336457.82, 327396.58]
  },
  "labels": ["Q2 - 2011", "Q3 - 2011", "Q4 - 2011", "Q1 - 2012",
    "Q2 - 2012", "Q3 - 2012"]
}
```

With the data sorted, we move on to updating the chart. To do this, we perform the following steps:

1. We start by including the `categoryAxisRenderer` plugin file along with the `barRenderer`, `trendline`, and `canvas` plugin files, as follows:

```
<script
  src="../js/jqplot.categoryAxisRenderer.min.js"></script>
<script src="../js/jqplot.barRenderer.min.js"></script>
<script
  src="../js/jqplot.canvasTextRenderer.min.js"></script>
<script
  src="../js/jqplot.canvasAxisTickRenderer.min.js"></script>
```

```
<script src="../js/jqplot.trendline.min.js"></script>
<script src="../js/functions.js"></script>
```

2. We declare an array to hold all the `series` objects we will create. We also
   create an array to hold our ticks. To build our `series` objects and the `tick`
   objects, we need to create a few helper functions. We start by creating a
   function called `createSeries`. We pass in the name of the category and the
   index of the category in our drop-down menu to select trend lines, as follows:

```
<script>
$(document).ready(function(){
  var dataSeriesObj = new Array;
  var ticks = new Array;
  function createSeries(name, index) {
```

3. Next, we create a variable to hold an object with the `label` and `trendline`
   options. To generate the `trendline` option, we will call `createTrendObj`,
   where we pass in the `name` and `index` parameters. Once this object is created,
   we return the entire `series` object, as shown in the following code snippet:

```
    var series = { label: name, trendline:
      createTrendObj(name, index) };
    return series;
  }
```

4. Our next function is `createTrendObj`. We create a variable to hold the
   `trendline` options. We set the `show` option to `false` by default. Then, we
   set the `label` option to include the category name, which is passed into the
   function as follows:

```
  function createTrendObj(name, index) {
    var trendLineObj = { show: false, label: 'Trend: ' +
      name };
```

5. Next, we check whether `index` matches the value of our drop-down menu.
   We also add a condition check that will show the trend line for the first
   category when the page is first loaded. Once the object is created, we return
   the object as follows:

```
    if (index == $("#trendline").val() || $("#trendline").val() ==
null) {
      trendLineObj.show = true;
    }
    return trendLineObj ;
  }
```

6. With the functions complete, we revisit our `dataPull` function. It will make use of the two functions we just created. We create a local variable to hold each data series. Next, we set `remoteData.categories` in a new variable called `categories`, so it will be easier to work with the objects inside our loop. As we did with other JSON objects, we loop through each object. We set the next element in `data` to the data array for the given object, as follows:

```
function dataPull(remoteData,options) {
  var data = new Array();
  var i = 0;
  var categories = remoteData.categories;
  for (var name in categories) {
    if (categories.hasOwnProperty(name)) {
      data[i] = categories[name];
```

7. Then, we call `createSeries` and store the resulting object in the next element of `dataSeriesObj`. The last thing in our loop through the categories is to create an `option` tag for our drop-down menu, as follows:

```
      dataSeriesObj[i] = createSeries(name,i);
      $("#trendline").append($("<option></option>")
        .attr("value",i).text(name));
      i++;
    }
  }
```

8. Once we are done with the loop, we set our previously declared variable `ticks` to `remoteData.labels`. With all of this data generated, we return the data points to jqPlot, as follows:

```
  ticks = remoteData.labels;
  return data;
}
```

9. With our remote data function complete, we create a function to be called each time we change the drop-down menu. Our `dataPull` function will pull all data and create `dataSeriesObj` and `ticks`. We set these options in our `replot` method, and the chart will reload as follows:

```
function refreshChart() {
  rev_category.replot( {
    series: dataSeriesObj,
    axes: { xaxis: { ticks: ticks } }
  });
}
```

10. Now we begin building our chart. We pass in the JSON URL to jqPlot. We pass in our functions for `dataRenderer` and `dataRendererOptions`, as follows:

```
var rev_category = $.jqplot ('rev_category', './data/quarterly_
revenue.json',
  {
    title:'Quarterly Revenue by Product Category',
    dataRenderer: remoteDataCallback,
    dataRendererOptions: { dataCallback: dataPull },
    axesDefaults: {
      tickRenderer: $.jqplot.CanvasAxisTickRenderer,
      tickOptions: { angle: -30 }
    },
```

11. We leave the `seriesDefaults` and `legend` options as they were before:

```
    seriesDefaults:{
      renderer:$.jqplot.BarRenderer,
      rendererOptions: {
        barMargin: 2,
        barPadding: 2,
        shadowAlpha: 0.0
      },
      trendline: { color: '#111111', lineWidth: 4 }
    },
    legend: { show: true, placement: 'outside', location:
      'ne' },
```

12. We need to pass in an array of objects to series. We also need to pass an array to the `ticks` option. If we load our chart as is, the `ticks` option will not appear. That is because jqPlot builds the chart before passing in the remote data:

```
    series: dataSeriesObj,
    axes:{
      xaxis:{
        label: 'Quarters',
        renderer: $.jqplot.CategoryAxisRenderer,
        ticks: ticks
      },
      yaxis: {
        label: 'Total in Dollars',
        padMax: 1,
        tickOptions: { formatString: "$%'d" }
      }
    }
  });
```

13. With our chart complete, we call the `refreshChart` method which will run the `replot` method and update the chart ticks with the newly created array of ticks:

```
refreshChart();
```

14. We change the entire event handler for the drop-down menu. We start by looping through `dataSeriesObj`. We call the `createTrendObj` function and reset the options for each `trendline` object. When we are done looping through the data series, we call `refreshChart` to reload the chart. This can be implemented as follows:

```
$("#trendline").change(function() {
  for(var x=0;x < dataSeriesObj.length; x++){
    dataSeriesObj[x].trendline =
createTrendObj(dataSeriesObj[x].label, x);
  }
  refreshChart();
});

});
</script>
```

15. We remove all the `option` tags from the drop-down menu because they will be generated dynamically:

```
<select id="trendline" name="trendline"></select>
<div id="rev_category" style="width:500px;"></div>
```

Finally, we load the chart in our browser; the result is shown in the following screenshot:

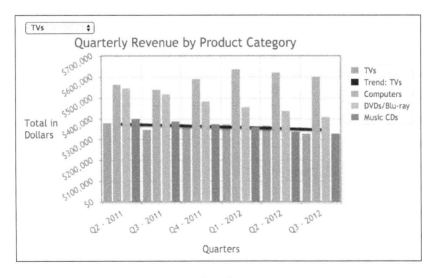

The advantage of our new chart is that in the next quarter, the new data will be loaded without us having to change the chart. Also, if in 2 months they decide to add new product categories to the JSON feed, they will appear without any changes on our part. If they add too many, however, the chart may become unusable, and we will have to evaluate different options to display the new data.

We select **DVDs/Blu-ray**, and the chart reloads without refreshing the page. The trend line for TVs is turned off, and it is enabled for DVDs/Blu-ray, as shown in the following screenshot:

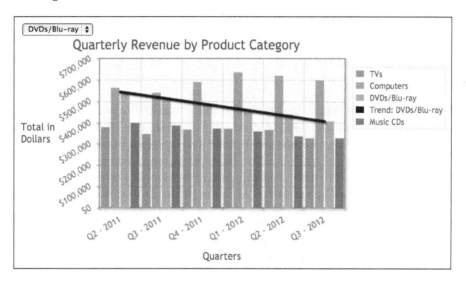

It's getting close to 4 o'clock. We begin to wrap up our charts and take care of e-mails and phone calls. About 15 minutes later, Roshan and Calvin stop by. Roshan tells us that Jeff mentioned the chart we created for him. We show it to him and Calvin. Roshan comments on the chart. "This is really nice. We'll have to think through how to best use this to increase sales in-store. This is beside the point, but this is a good first step. I also heard you two were thinking in the same vein as I was to get live data for several of these charts."

We show him the updated product category chart and the updated stock chart. "These are really nice. These are actually two of the charts we discussed in our meeting earlier. The team is going to want some of these on the dashboard when we go live. It's late in the day, but I wanted to stop by and schedule a meeting for Monday. We have the charts and the data. Now, we need to make it all beautiful and fit together in a cohesive way."

Calvin speaks up, "We'll see you two on Monday. Have a good weekend." Calvin and Roshan turn and leave. We finish the few last e-mails, and then head out ourselves.

Learning questions

1. What is the difference between the `redraw` and `replot` methods?

2. Why did we have to call the `replot` method immediately after we created our bar chart?

3. What are some of the possible pitfalls of having our charts generated based on remote data sources?

4. What are some of the options we used for our meter gauge?

5. Most of our charts are based on predetermined datasets. What issues might arise if the amount of data returned is unlimited?

Summary

We looked at a new chart type that is similar to a gauge on a car dashboard. We also used the `redraw` and `replot` methods to update this chart at intervals. We changed the time frame for our stock chart and updated the data source being used. We created our `ticks` option based on remote data and updated our chart using `replot`. We also used this same functionality to change the trend line displayed based on the selected value in our drop-down menu.

In the next chapter, we'll look at some of the styling options that can be set using CSS and other options that can only be set via JavaScript. We will also look at creating themes for jqPlot using JavaScript objects.

10
Beautifying and Extending Your Charts

In each of the previous chapters, we have looked at new chart types or plugins that augmented the functionality of our charts. In this chapter, we will look at how to style the grid and create themed charts. We will also create reusable functions to simplify the building of our charts. In this chapter, we will cover the following topics:

- Change the background color of the grid and remove all the grid lines
- Discuss how the `canvas` element in HTML works and the proper way to style it
- Create a line chart using the second `xaxis` and smoothing lines
- Create a waterfall chart and set the negative colors to match our company's color scheme
- Create functions to build plot objects with default options for a bar chart
- Use our newly-created functions to build bar charts with less code

Nailing down the charts for our dashboard

We get into the office around 9 o'clock and head to the conference room for our meeting with Roshan. A few minutes later he and Calvin arrive. "Thanks for joining us this morning," Roshan begins. "I think we've settled on the charts we want on the dashboard. We've decided we want two versions: one for vice presidents that give a company-wide view and one for managers to keep abreast of their divisions."

Roshan continues, "I think the next step for you two will be to modify the charts to match our brand standards. For the company-wide charts, we want to use the company's purple color scheme. For each division, we want the red, green, and blue color schemes. Is there any way we can use a different color for the background of the charts? If so, let's make it a lighter version of the standard color. The tan or off-white color is just bland. Beyond changing the background color, we'll leave it to you to find other ways to put some polish on the charts."

The meeting wraps up and we gather our things. Calvin speaks up, "I forgot to bring the list of which charts go with which report. I'll e-mail that over when I get back to my office." We head back to our office and work through our e-mails from the weekend. About 10 minutes later, we get an e-mail from Calvin. It lists the following charts for the company-wide report:

- The stacked bar chart showing the last 12 months of divisional revenue
- The waterfall chart showing expenses against revenue
- The line chart showing the last 12 months of revenue and profit
- The bar chart showing product return reasons

Thankfully, we already have a working version of each chart. We just need to clean them up and style them.

Changing the background color of our chart

We start with the line chart showing profit and revenue because it is the simplest. We open our previous chart, `1168_01_06.html`, and save it as a new file. We now have a remote data source with the revenue and profit numbers. We check the URL and find an object for both revenue and profit. Each object contains an array of arrays with the date as the x value and the dollar amount as the y value, as shown in the following code snippet:

```
{
  "Revenue": [
    ["2011-11-20", 800538],
    . . .
  ],
  "Profit": [
    ["2011-11-20", 192049.56],
      . . .
  ]
}
```

1. We start by adding the `functions.js` script so that we can use `remoteDataCallback` to pull the revenue and profit numbers. We create our `dataPull` function and return the `revenue` and `profit` arrays wrapped in another array as follows:

```
<script src="../js/jqplot.dateAxisRenderer.min.js"></script>
<script src="../js/functions.js"></script>
<script>
$(document).ready(function(){
  function dataPull(remoteData,options) {
    return [remoteData.Revenue, remoteData.Profit];
  }
```

2. We set the data source to our JSON feed and set `dataRenderer` and `dataRendererOptions` with the same options we've used with our previous charts that use remote sources. We also set the labels for each series and set the `Profit` series to appear on `y2axis` as follows:

```
  var rev_profit = $.jqplot ('revenueProfitChart', 'data/12_month_
rev_profit.json',
  {
    title:'Monthly Revenue & Profit',
    dataRenderer: remoteDataCallback,
    dataRendererOptions: { dataCallback: dataPull },
    series:[
        { label: 'Revenue' },
        { label: 'Profit', yaxis:'y2axis' }
    ],
```

3. We create our legend and set the `xaxis` to use `DateAxisRenderer` and format our two *y* axes to format the strings as currency. We also use the `alignTicks` option on our second `yaxis`. This will cause the ticks and gridlines for `yaxis` and `y2axis` to line up and make a better looking chart as follows:

```
    legend: { show: true, placement: 'outsideGrid' },
    axes:{
        xaxis:{ renderer:$.jqplot.DateAxisRenderer },
        yaxis:{ tickOptions: { formatString: "$%'d" } },
        y2axis:{
          rendererOptions: { alignTicks: true },
          tickOptions: { formatString: "$%'d" }
        }
    }
  });
});
</script>
```

4. We want the background to be purple but with a low opacity. We create a class in `styles.css` called `purple_bg` and set the background color to `rgba(64,0,64,0.25)`. We also create a class to set the width of our chart to 700 pixels as follows:

```
<div id="revenueProfitChart" class="purple_bg w700"></div>
```

We load the chart in our browser, where we can already see an issue with the background color. It must be a Monday morning.

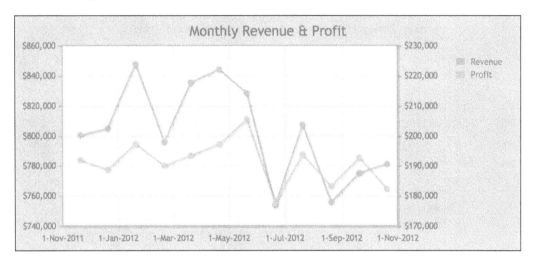

Canvas versus CSS

jqPlot uses a combination of HTML styled by CSS and canvas elements added to the HTML. Canvas elements are created using JavaScript and jqPlot simplifies the creation of these canvas elements. When it creates a plot, it creates several different canvas elements. A separate canvas element is created for each series along with an element for the grid. If our lines or bars have shadows, there is an element for each shadow. Also, if we use the canvas renderers for our ticks or labels, those are created as canvas elements.

In the past, we modified the default jqPlot CSS styles for our legend, tooltips, and ticks. This is thanks to jqPlot creating divs or tables that we can alter using CSS styling. However, with canvas elements, the only thing we can change with CSS is the positioning of the entire canvas or change the display status. Our shadows, lines, bars, and rotated ticks are drawn on the canvas using JavaScript and, just like a painting, each piece is now part of the whole and cannot be removed or changed using CSS.

With this understanding, we find the `grid` element where we can set the background color, turn off grid lines, and other options:

1. We turn back to the code. We want to rotate the ticks of our axes, so we include those plugin files as follows:

```
<script
    src="../js/jqplot.canvasTextRenderer.min.js"></script>
<script
    src="../js/jqplot.canvasAxisTickRenderer.min.js"></script>
```

2. Next, we set the `grid` option and start by setting `backgroundColor` to `rgba(64,0,64,0.25)`. We set `gridLineColor` to `#fff` because the default gray color will be hard to see. We also set `borderColor` to `#000` to add contrast. We set `tickRenderer` and `tickOptions` under `axesDefaults` as follows:

```
grid: {
    backgroundColor: 'rgba(64,0,64,0.25)',
    gridLineColor: '#fff',
    borderColor: '#000'
},
...
axesDefaults: {
    tickRenderer: $.jqplot.CanvasAxisTickRenderer,
    tickOptions: { angle: -30 }
```

3. There are a few extra options under our `xaxis` that we want to change. We set `showGridline` to `false` so that only the `yaxes` grid lines will appear. We also set the angle for our ticks to be a little steeper as follows:

```
axes:{
    xaxis:{
        renderer:$.jqplot.DateAxisRenderer,
        tickOptions: {
            formatString: "%b %Y",
            showGridline: false,
            angle: -45
        }
    },
```

4. We finish by creating classes to make the width and height of our div smaller so that it fits on our dashboard better:

```
<div id="revenueProfitChart" class="w500 h250"></div>
```

We load the chart and view the results; we are making progress, but we've also introduced some formatting problems. The title is being centered to the entire `canvas` element and not the rendered chart, so it is out of alignment as shown in the following screenshot:

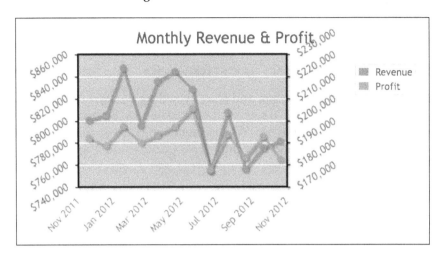

We've also been thinking about this line chart. The lines do not show actual values in between our markers. We can use the smooth option which will round out the lines. This way they will appear more as decoration than denoting intervening increases or decreases between our markers.

Using the second xaxis and smoothing lines

We save the previous chart as a new file and begin making our modifications as follows:

1. We want an array containing various shades of the purple used by the company. We can use these colors for our lines, bars, pie wedges, and even our backgrounds. We also want this in a central place along with the functions to help us theme our charts. With that in mind, we create a file called `themes.js` and add an array called `company_colors` to hold our shades of purple as follows:

    ```
    var company_colors = [ "#400040", "#8C008C", "#D8BFD8", "#DE6FA1",
    "#9400D3" ];
    ```

2. Next, we return to our file containing our HTML, `1168_10_03.html`. We include the `themes.js` file in our HTML. After setting `dataRendererOptions`, we set `seriesDefaults`. Inside this object, we set `rendererOptions` and then set `smooth` to `true`. We also set `seriesColors` to the `company_colors` array in `themes.js` as follows:

```
<script src="../js/themes.js"></script>
...
  dataRendererOptions: { dataCallback: dataPull },
  seriesDefaults: { rendererOptions: { smooth: true } },
  seriesColors: company_colors,
```

3. We removed the grid lines for the `xaxis` in our previous version. Now, we want to turn off the border at the top and bottom of our chart. We will need to set `borderWidth` to `0` for both `x2axis` and `xaxis`. The `yaxis` appears on the left of our chart and `y2axis` appears on the right. Since `xaxis` is at the bottom of our chart, `x2axis` corresponds to the top of our chart. So by setting these options, the border at the top and bottom of our chart will disappear. This can be implemented as follows:

```
axes:{
  x2axis: { borderWidth: 0 },
  xaxis:{
    renderer:$.jqplot.DateAxisRenderer,
    borderWidth: 0,
```

4. Finally, we create a rule in `styles.css` using the `.jqplot-title` selector. Our title is being centered to the entire chart div and it doesn't look right. We move it to the left to make it look like it is centered over the drawn chart:

```
#purpleRevenueProfit .jqplot-title {
  left: -55px !important;
}
```

We refresh the chart in our browser. Now, the lines match the company color scheme and they are curved:

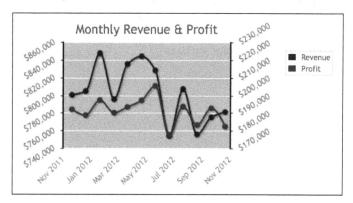

We have gotten the revenue and profit chart to a good point. We decide to move on to the waterfall chart.

Setting negative colors on a bar chart

Just as there is a default array of colors for data series in jqPlot, there is a separate array of colors used for negative values. We want the color of the negative bars in our waterfall chart to match our color scheme. We also want to modify the layout of the chart. We open our previous waterfall chart, `1168_08_03.html`, as a new file and begin making the following modifications:

1. We add in `themes.js` and create a version of the `dataPull` function to pass each JSON object to our data array. We also connect the data to our remote JSON feed as follows:

```
<script src="../js/themes.js"></script>
<script>
$(document).ready(function(){
   function dataPull(rd,options) {
     return [[rd.revenue,
       rd.operating_expenses,
       rd.fixed_costs,
       rd.returns]];
   }

   var waterFall = $.jqplot ('waterFall', 'data/revenue_expenses.
json',
     {
```

2. We set `backgroundColor` for our grid and set the options to pull our remote data. We also set `seriesColors` to use `company_colors`, which is located in `themes.js` as follows:

```
grid: { backgroundColor: 'rgba(64,0,64,0.25)' },
dataRenderer: remoteDataCallback,
dataRendererOptions: { dataCallback: dataPull },
seriesColors: company_colors,
```

3. In `themes.js`, we create a new variable to hold our array of negative colors. We make a copy of `company_colors` and then reverse the array. It looks like the following line of code:

```
n_company_colors = company_colors.slice(0).reverse();
```

4. We return to our HTML file and assign our new array `n_company_colors` to `negativeSeriesColors` as follows:

```
negativeSeriesColors: n_company_colors,
```

5. Since our point labels are formatted as currency, we can remove the `ticks` and `axis` label by setting `showTicks` and `showLabel` to `false`. We also set `showGridline` to `false` as shown in the following code snippet:

```
axes:{
  y2axis:{
    showTicks: false,
    showLabel: false,
    min: 0,
    tickOptions: { formatString: "$%'d", showGridline: false }
  },
```

6. We finish by adding an `h2` tag for our title and by adding classes to our chart div to decrease its width and height as follows:

```
<h2>Expenses Against Revenue - Last 12 Months</h2>
<div id="purpleWaterFall" class="w400 h300"></div>
```

7. We then move over to `styles.css`. We add the following rule to make the background of our point labels more opaque and increase readability:

```
#purpleWaterFall .jqplot-point-label {
  background: rgba(255,255,255,.8);
  border: 1px solid #999;
  padding:0px 3px;
}
```

We pull up the chart in our browser and see that it is still easy to understand even after removing the ticks from the *y* axis. The various shades of purple also work well as shown in the following screenshot:

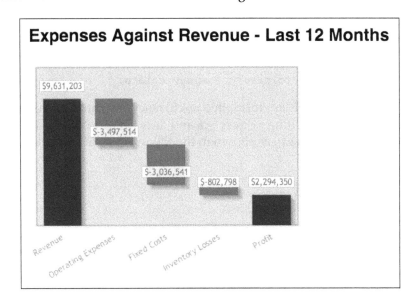

We have removed unnecessary parts and changed the style so that it no longer looks like the bar charts we originally created. With the `ticks` and `point` labels of the *x* axis alone, we are able to tell a clear story.

We look up from our code and realize that it's lunch time. We are at a good spot to stop so we head to the sandwich shop down the street. We enjoy a long lunch and get back to the office ready to finish up our new charts.

Creating reusable plot objects

We begin to prepare everything for our next chart, but we stop ourselves. Our last two charts for the VPs are bar charts and have very similar options. Several of the charts for the divisional managers could use the same code but with a different data source.

You mention we should DRY up our code. I give you a look. You continue by telling me it means, "Don't Repeat Yourself." I continue to look at you with slight bewilderment. "What?" you say, "I've been reading *The Pragmatic Programmer*."

This is sound advice. There may be a bit more up-front work to create these objects, but the savings in time and energy for each subsequent chart will be worth it.

We look back at our existing bar charts and distill the most common options. We open `themes.js` so we can get started creating an object to contain our default settings:

1. We start by creating the `defaultBarObj` variable as a function expression. This means we'll store an unnamed function in a variable. We will pass in `seriesObj`, the renderer object for our *x* axis and `dataPull`. We can't pass in a named function called `dataPull` because we can't store a regular function into our object. So, we'll change our function to an expression and store it in a variable named `dataPull`. The creation of `defaultBarObj` is as follows:

   ```
   var defaultBarObj = function(seriesObj, renderer, dataPull) {
   ```

2. Inside our function, we create `barObj` to hold all our options. We can reuse the options that would normally be set within our jqPlot object. We set `dataCallback` to our new variable `dataPull`. Our code to pull remote data will work as before. We also set our `seriesDefaults` as follows:

   ```
   var barObj = {
     dataRenderer: remoteDataCallback,
     dataRendererOptions: { dataCallback: dataPull },
     seriesDefaults:{
       renderer:$.jqplot.BarRenderer,
       rendererOptions: {
         barMargin: 5,
         barPadding: 5
       }
     },
   ```

3. On the initial build, `seriesObj` will be empty but will be populated when `dataPull` is called. We set `axesDefaults` to use `CanvasAxisTickRenderer`. We want our ticks to be black instead of gray, so we set `textColor` to black. Again, we can't use CSS to style ticks that are rendered as canvas elements:

   ```
   series: seriesObj,
   axesDefaults: {
     tickRenderer: $.jqplot.CanvasAxisTickRenderer,
     tickOptions: {
       angle: -30,
       textColor: '#000'
     }
   },
   ```

4. Since we can use either dates or categories on our *x* axis, we will pass in the jqPlot `renderer` object. Most of our charts deal with currency so we set `formatString` to format those values properly. We can always override any of these values later:

```
axes:{
  xaxis:{ renderer: renderer },
  yaxis: {
    min: 0,
    tickOptions: { formatString: "$%'d" }
  }
},
```

5. We include a legend and then return the entire object.

```
  legend: { show: true, placement: 'outside', location:
    'e' }
};

return barObj;
};
```

6. Our function `defaultBarObj` handles most of the structure for our chart. We also create a function called `color_theme`. We'll pass in the object created by `defaultBarObj` and also an array of colors. This can be the `company_colors` array or the color arrays for our divisions that we'll create in a bit. We set `seriesColors` to the `colors` array we pass in as follows:

```
var color_theme = function(obj,colors) {
  obj.seriesColors = colors;
```

7. Next, we set the `grid` options. Instead of storing a separate background color, we will just use the first color in our `colors` array. We also want to change the opacity of the background, so we use the `hex2rgb` method in jqPlot. It will return the converted color and opacity in `rgba` notation. After this, we turn off the grid lines and the shadow and set the border color to black:

```
obj.grid = {
  backgroundColor: $.jqplot.hex2rgb(colors[0], 0.1),
  drawGridlines: false,
  shadow: false,
  borderColor: '#000'
};

return obj;
};
```

8. Now that we have our theming function, we need an object with colors for each division. Since most of our remote JSON data matches this format, we can pull an array of colors based on which division is returned in our JSON as follows:

```
division_colors = {
  "Nerd Corral": [ "#00007F", "#0BA2D6", "#40407F" ],
  "Media/Software": [ "#6B7F6F", "#007F19", "#69FF86", "#A1BFA7",
"#0DFF66"],
  "Electronics": [ "#7F0000", "#FF0000", "#FF7F7F", "#7F6666",
"#4C2626"]
};
```

With this complete, all our default options are set in objects that we can include when creating our charts. This will greatly shorten the amount of code needed to create our charts.

Using objects to piece together our chart

We both sit back a bit exhausted. That was a lot of work but now is when we'll see the pay-off. With all these functions created, we start with the stacked bar chart showing total revenue for each division. We decide to start from scratch with our HTML since we are completely changing how we build our chart.

1. We add the `dateAxisRenderer`, `barRenderer`, and `canvas` plugin files. We also make sure to add `functions.js` and `themes.js`:

```
<script src="../js/jqplot.dateAxisRenderer.js"></script>
<script src="../js/jqplot.barRenderer.min.js"></script>
<script
  src="../js/jqplot.canvasTextRenderer.min.js"></script>
<script
  src="../js/jqplot.canvasAxisTickRenderer.min.js"></script>
<script src="../js/functions.js"></script>
<script src="../js/themes.js"></script>
<script>
$(document).ready(function(){
```

2. Next, we create `dataSeriesObj` to hold the options for each series. Instead of creating our normal `dataPull` function, we create another function expression. We loop through each division and store the values in `data`. We create an object where we set the `label` to the division name stored in `division`. We also set the color for the series to the element in `division_colors` that matches the currently selected division. When we finish our loop, we return our data array as shown in the following code snippet:

```
var dataSeriesObj = new Array;

var dataPull = function(remoteData,options) {
  var data = new Array();
  for (var division in remoteData) {
    if (remoteData.hasOwnProperty(division)) {
      data.push(remoteData[division]);
      dataSeriesObj.push( { label: division, color: division_
colors[division][0] } );
    }
  }
  return data;
};
```

3. We declare `plotObj` to hold the object that `defaultBarObj` will return. We pass in our empty `dataSeriesObj` array, the date plugin, and our new `dataPull` function expression. Our default structure only creates basic bar charts, so we set `stackSeries` to `true` on our new `plotObj`. We also add our title as follows:

```
var plotObj = defaultBarObj(dataSeriesObj, $.jqplot.
DateAxisRenderer, dataPull);
  plotObj.stackSeries = true;
  plotObj.title = 'Monthly Revenue by Division';
```

4. We also format the ticks on `xaxis` to show the month and year. We finish building our object by passing `plotObj` and `company_colors` into `color_theme`. This will set `seriesColors` to our purple array, which creates the default series colors. When `dataPull` is called, the color for each series is overwritten as follows:

```
plotObj.axes.xaxis.tickOptions = { formatString: "%b %Y" };
  plotObj = color_theme(plotObj,company_colors);
```

5. Normally, we create a long list of object variables, but since these are all stored in `plotObj`, we just pass that into our jqPlot object. Because we are creating everything as an object and passing in `dataPull` as a variable, `dataSeriesObj` is updated before the chart is rendered. Therefore, our series labels and colors are available when the chart is rendered, so we won't have to call `replot` like we did with our charts last week.

```
    var division_revenue = $.jqplot ('division_revenue',
'data/12_
month_div_revenue.json', plotObj);
    });
    </script>
```

6. We set the width and height so that it will fit better on a page with multiple charts as follows:

```
<div id="purpleDivisionRevenue" class="w400 h300"></div>
```

We load the chart in our browser and review the results. We have a stacked bar chart where each division is rendered in its own respective color scheme. Also, we removed the grid lines and the background is based on the company color scheme as shown in the following screenshot:

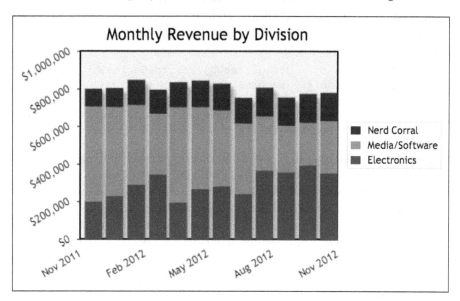

Reaping the benefits of the DRY code

We have one more chart to create for the VP's dashboard in the form of a bar chart showing product returns. We were able to get the data for each return category for the last 12 months in a JSON feed. We can reuse `defaultBarObj` and `color_theme`, which will speed up the building of our chart as follows:

1. We open the chart we created a few weeks ago, `1168_03_05.html`. Since all of these charts are going to be combined into one page, we need to create separate variables for our series objects and our functions to format the remote data as follows:

```
$(document).ready(function(){
  var returnsSeriesObj = [];
  var returnsDataPull = function(remoteData,options) {
    return [remoteData];
  };
```

2. We pass in our new series object, `CategoryAxisRenderer`, and our new `returnsDataPull` function. Once we create `returnsPlotObj`, we set `varyBarColor` to `true`. Our first version of this chart had the same color for each bar since they are technically all in the same series. Using `varyBarColor` will alternate between each of the colors we pass into `seriesColors`. We also turn on `pointLabels` as follows:

```
var returnsPlotObj = defaultBarObj(returnsSeriesObj, $.jqplot.
CategoryAxisRenderer, returnsDataPull);
returnsPlotObj.title = 'Last 12 Months of Product Returns';
returnsPlotObj.seriesDefaults.rendererOptions.varyBarColor = true;
returnsPlotObj.seriesDefaults.pointLabels = { show: true };
```

3. We set `yaxis.padMax` to `1.5` so all of our point labels will stay within the chart. We also turn off the ticks and labels for our `yaxis`. Since we only have one series, we also set `show` to `false` to turn off our legend. We finish creating our chart options by passing in our `returnsPlotObj` and `company_colors` into `color_theme` to style our chart. After that we build our chart using our options stored in `returnsPlotObj` as follows:

```
returnsPlotObj.axes.yaxis.padMax = 1.5;
returnsPlotObj.axes.yaxis.showTicks = false;
returnsPlotObj.legend.show = false;
returnsPlotObj = color_theme(returnsPlotObj,company_colors);

var product_returns = $.jqplot ('product_returns', 'data/
returns.json', returnsPlotObj);
});
</script>
<div id="purpleProductReturns"></div>
```

4. We create a rule in `styles.css` to add some margin to the left of our chart. Now, we will be able to see all of our rotated labels on the *x* axis since we turned off the labels on the *y* axis. The code to implement this is as follows:

```
#purpleProductReturns {
  margin-left: 30px;
  width: 400px;
  color: #000;
}
```

We load the chart and see the bars alternate in color. Also, the point labels make up for the lack of labels on the *y* axis as shown in the following screenshot:

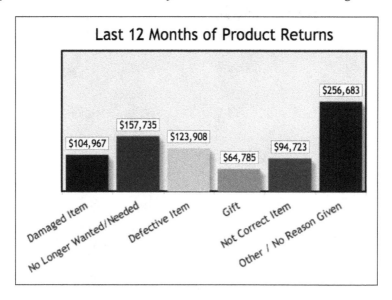

We have updated the four charts we need for the VP dashboard and it is 5 o'clock. Tomorrow morning, we'll take everything we've done today and merge it into one HTML file.

Learning questions

1. What is the term that is used to describe a function stored in a variable?

2. What does DRY mean?

3. How much styling can we do on a `canvas` element with CSS?

4. What is the order of precedence for setting colors for a series?

5. What else could we do to streamline our code?

Summary

We started this chapter by looking at how canvas elements work. We discussed what parts of a jqPlot chart can be modified using CSS and which have to be modified by JavaScript on the canvas. We looked at the x2axis element and how to smooth lines. We also changed the default colors for negative numbers within our series.

We then created a function expression to create default options for our bar charts. Then with our default options set, we passed the object into another function to style our charts. With all this up-front work, it reduced the amount of code needed and also reduced the development time for each subsequent chart.

In the next chapter, we will combine all of these charts into one document. We will also look at modifying one of the rendering plugins for jqPlot.

11
Bringing it All Together

Over the course of this book, we have covered various options for the creation and styling of charts. All of this hard work and learning will culminate in the projects that we will create in this chapter. In this chapter, we'll learn the following topics:

- Combine the four charts from the previous chapter into a coherent dashboard
- Build a divisional dashboard based on the division submitted through a query string
- Create a chart and mix the line renderer with the bar renderer
- Add our company logo to our mixed chart using a `canvas` element
- Modify the donut renderer plugin to add a tooltip
- Modify our donut chart to use our modified donut plugin

We return to the office on Tuesday morning to finish up the VP dashboard and show it off to Roshan, Sara, and Calvin. All we need to do is take the charts we made yesterday and convert a few of the `dataPull` functions to the function expressions and create unique names for the objects holding the plot options and the series data.

Combining four charts into a dashboard

We created four charts yesterday and now we need to merge these into one page. We create a new file and save it. To combine the four charts into a dashboard, perform the following steps:

1. We start by adding in all the plugin files we need for all four charts:

```
<script src="../js/jqplot.dateAxisRenderer.min.js"></script>
<script src="../js/jqplot.categoryAxisRenderer.min.js"></script>
<script src="../js/jqplot.barRenderer.min.js"></script>
<script src="../js/jqplot.pointLabels.min.js"></script>
<script src="../js/jqplot.canvasTextRenderer.min.js"></script>
```

```
<script src="../js/jqplot.canvasAxisTickRenderer.min.js"></script>
<script src="../js/functions.js"></script>
<script src="../js/themes.js"></script>
```

2. Next, we paste in the JavaScript for our line chart from `1168_10_03.html`. We start by changing the name of our `dataPull` function to `profitDataPull` as follows:

```
var profitDataPull = function(remoteData,options) {
    return [remoteData.Revenue, remoteData.Profit];
}
```

3. We could create a default line chart object, but since there are so many custom changes, we would spend more time overwriting our defaults. So, we only change the name of the function under `dataRendererOptions` as follows:

```
dataRendererOptions: { dataCallback: profitDataPull },
```

4. Next, we copy over the JavaScript for our waterfall chart found in `1168_10_04.html`. We create a function expression unique for our waterfall chart as follows:

```
var revExpDataPull = function(rd,options) {
    return [[rd.revenue,
        rd.operating_expenses,
        rd.fixed_costs,
        rd.returns]];
}
```

5. We make use of our default bar chart object and save this in our `revExpPlotObj` variable also passing in our new `revExpDataPull` function. We set `negativeSeriesColors` to `n_company_colors`. Under `rendererOptions` for our series defaults, we set `waterfall` and `useNegativeColors` to `true` and `highlightMouseOver` to `false` as shown in the following code snippet:

```
var revExpPlotObj = defaultBarObj(revExpSeriesObj, $.jqplot.
CategoryAxisRenderer, revExpDataPull);
    revExpPlotObj.negativeSeriesColors = n_company_colors;
    revExpPlotObj.seriesDefaults.rendererOptions = {
        waterfall: true,
        useNegativeColors: true,
        highlightMouseOver: false
    };
```

6. We also set `pointLabels` to `true` and turn off the *y* axis ticks and the legend as follows:

```
revExpPlotObj.seriesDefaults.pointLabels = { show: true };
revExpPlotObj.axes.yaxis.showTicks = false;
revExpPlotObj.legend.show = false;
revExpPlotObj.axes.xaxis.ticks = ['Revenue', 'Operating
Expenses', 'Fixed Costs', 'Inventory Losses', 'Profit'];
revExpPlotObj.axes.xaxis.tickOptions = { showGridline: false,
showMark: false };
```

7. We finish by using `color_theme` to modify the grid and then we create our chart using the following code:

```
revExpPlotObj = color_theme(revExpPlotObj,company_colors);


var waterFall = $.jqplot ('purpleWaterFall', 'data/revenue_
expenses.json', revExpPlotObj);
```

8. For our divisional revenue chart, we start by creating an array to hold our series objects. We also want to use the category renderer instead of the date renderer, so we need an array to hold our ticks. This can be implemented as follows:

```
var divisionSeriesObj = [], divisionTicks = [];
```

9. Now, we create a function to pull our remote data. We start by looping through each division in the `remoteData` object as follows:

```
var divisionDataPull = function(remoteData,options) {
  var data = [], i = 0;
  for (var division in remoteData) {
```

10. Next, we loop through each array within the division object. We add that to our data array and add the date to our `divisionTicks` array as follows:

```
if (remoteData.hasOwnProperty(division)) {
  data[i] = [];
  for(var x=0;x<remoteData[division].length;x++) {
    data[i].push(remoteData[division][x][1]);
    divisionTicks[x] = remoteData[division][x][0];
  }
```

11. Once we have our data and the ticks created, we then create the series object and add that to the divisionSeriesObj array. Once we have looped through all the divisions, we return the data array as follows:

```
        divisionSeriesObj.push( {
          label: division,
          color: division_colors[division][0]
        } );
        i++;
      }
    }
    return data;
  };
```

12. Next, we create an object to hold our chart settings and pass in our new function, divisionDataPull. We set the ticks to use our new tick array and create the chart by passing in divisionPlotObj as shown in the following code snippet:

```
  var divisionPlotObj = defaultBarObj(divisionSeriesObj, $.jqplot.
CategoryAxisRenderer, divisionDataPull);
  divisionPlotObj.stackSeries = true;
  divisionPlotObj.axes.xaxis.ticks = divisionTicks;
  divisionPlotObj = color_theme( divisionPlotObj, company_colors
);


  var division_revenue = $.jqplot ('purpleDivisionRevenue',
'data/12_month_div_revenue.json', divisionPlotObj);
```

13. For our product returns chart found in 1168_10_06.html, we copy in the JavaScript without making any changes. With that out of the way, we move on to modifying the HTML for our charts. We wrap each chart div and h2 elements in a section tag as follows:

```
<section>
<h2>Monthly Revenue & Profit</h2>
<div id="purpleRevenueProfit" class="w500 h250"></div>
</section>
<section>
<h2>Expenses Against Revenue - Last 12 Months</h2>
<div id="purpleWaterFall" class="w400 h300"></div>
</section>
<section>
<h2>Monthly Revenue by Division</h2>
<div id="purpleDivisionRevenue" class="w400 h300"></div>
</section>
<section>
```

```
<h2>Last 12 Months of Product Returns</h2>
<div id="purpleProductReturns"></div>
</section>
```

14. With the HTML complete, we create a style rule in `styles.css` to float the `section` elements to the left and set their `min-width` to `48%` as shown in the following code snippet:

```
section {
  float: left;
  min-width: 48%;
}
```

With all that complete, we load the new page in our browser. This dashboard is a culmination of the last few weeks of work. The first two charts appear side-by-side and the other two wrap to the next line. The charts showing company-wide data use the company color scheme we created. The chart showing divisional revenue uses the colors for each division:

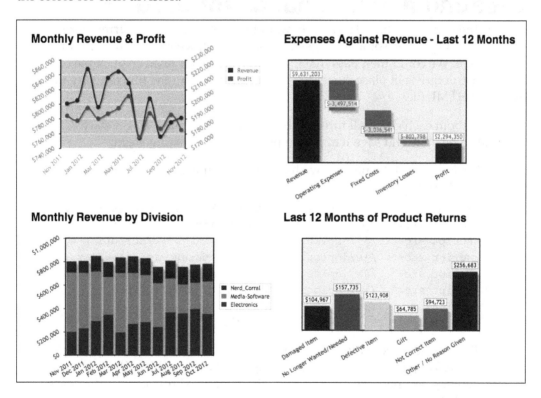

Each chart is compact but easy to read. It meets the goal of being a dashboard, something that a person can digest at a glance.

We call Calvin and ask him to schedule a quick review with Roshan and Sara.

"That will take some time," Calvin says. "While I'm getting everyone together, you could start on the divisional dashboard. I've got the list of charts the vice-presidents want for it."

We hear Calvin moving papers around, "Here we are. They want a stacked bar chart showing product revenue. They also want the product returns chart broken out by region. Finally, they want a separate product revenue chart with a trend line. They also want a drop-down option to change the trend line for the selected product category."

We tell him we'll get started on it while he contacts Roshan and Sara.

Creating a divisional dashboard

For the divisional dashboards, we only want to show data for the current user's division. Ideally, when someone logs in to the intranet, we would know his or her division. We could then pass that information into our JavaScript. None of that infrastructure is in place currently, so we will mock up the functionality in our static HTML files.

Thinking about each chart, all three of them will be bar charts. To get started, we create a new file and save it and then perform the following steps:

1. We include all the plugins we have used previously for our bar charts as follows:

   ```
   <script src="../js/jqplot.categoryAxisRenderer.min.js"></script>
   <script src="../js/jqplot.barRenderer.min.js"></script>
   <script src="../js/jqplot.pointLabels.min.js"></script>
   <script src="../js/jqplot.canvasTextRenderer.min.js"></script>
   <script src="../js/jqplot.canvasAxisTickRenderer.min.js"></script>
   <script src="../js/jqplot.trendline.min.js"></script>
   <script src="../js/functions.js"></script>
   <script src="../js/themes.js"></script>
   ```

2. To fake the server-side passing of the user's division, we use a query string value. We pass this value to the `h1` tag so we know which division we are viewing. We perform a `replace` method because browsers handle spaces in URLs in varying ways as follows:

   ```
   $(document).ready(function(){
   ```

```
    var selDivision = (getQueryStringVar('division')) || "Media-
Software";
    $("#division_name").html(selDivision.replace("_"," "));
```

3. We begin with the individual product categories chart with trend lines and it will be a bar chart. We create the array to hold our series data and our ticks. The first version of this chart had one function to create the `series` options and one to create the `trendline` options. We combine all that into one function as follows:

```
//****** Individual Categories with Trends *********/
var prodTrendSeriesObj = [], prodTrendTicks = [];

function createSeries(name, seriesIndex) {
  var series = {
    label: name,
    trendline: {
      show: false,
      label: 'Trend: ' + name
    }
  };
  if(seriesIndex== $("
    #trendline").val() ||
    ($("#trendline").val() ==
    null && index == 0)) {
      series.trendline.show = true;
    }
  return series;
}
```

4. Next, we create a function to take the selected division and loop through each product category, create our series objects, and add options to our drop-down menu. This function will be called from within the remote data function, `prodTrendDataPull`, as shown in the following code snippet:

```
function createSelDivision(prod_cat) {
  var i = 0, data = [];
  $.each( prod_cat, function( key, value ) {
    data[i] = prod_cat[key];
    prodTrendSeriesObj[i] = createSeries(key,i);
    $("#trendline").append("<option value=" + i + ">" + key +
"</option>");
    i++;
  });
  return data;
}
```

5. In our data formatting function, prodTrendDataPull, we loop through each category. If it matches selDivision, we call createSelDivision. We finish by looping through remoteData.labels and pushing these to the prodTrendTicks array as follows:

```
var prodTrendDataPull = function(remoteData,options) {
  var data = [], divisions = remoteData.divisions;
  for (var div in divisions) {
    if (divisions.hasOwnProperty(div)) {
      if(selDivision == div) {
        data = createSelDivision(divisions[div]);
      }
    }
  }
  $.each(remoteData.labels, function( i, value ) {
    prodTrendTicks.push(value);
  });
  return data;
};
```

6. We create refreshChart to be called each time the value in the drop-down menu is changed. We set seriesColors to the selected division_colors and set the *x* axis ticks to prodTrendTicks as follows:

```
function refreshChart() {
  rev_category.replot( {
    series: prodTrendSeriesObj,
    seriesColors: division_colors[selDivision],
    grid: { backgroundColor: getBgColor(
      division_colors[selDivision])},
    axes: { xaxis: { ticks: prodTrendTicks } }
  });
}
```

7. Since this chart is a bar chart, we create an object to hold our default plot options. In addition, we set the defaults for our trend line and enable the legend for this chart. We finalize our options by using color_theme to set the default colors to the company colors as follows:

```
var prodTrendPlotObj = defaultBarObj(prodTrendSeriesObj,
$.jqplot.CategoryAxisRenderer, prodTrendDataPull);
  prodTrendPlotObj.seriesDefaults.trendline = { color: '#000',
lineWidth: 4 };
  prodTrendPlotObj.legend = { show: true, placement:
'outsideGrid', location: 'ne' }
  prodTrendPlotObj = color_theme( prodTrendPlotObj, company_colors
);
```

8. We create our chart object using our JSON feed and our object `prodTrendPlotObj`. Since jqPlot creates the ticks before it pulls the data, we need to call `refreshChart` to update the ticks and the colors. This can be implemented as follows:

```
var rev_category = $.jqplot ('division_rev_category', './data/6_
month_prod_categories.json', prodTrendPlotObj);
refreshChart();
```

9. Previously, we called a function to set `trendline` options from within our drop-down event handler. Since we did away with that function, we add an if/else statement and set `trendline.show` to `true` or `false` for each series as follows:

```
$("#trendline").change(function() {
  var trendObj = prodTrendSeriesObj;
  for(var x=0; x < trendObj.length; x++){
    if(x == $(this).val()) {
      trendObj[x].trendline.show = true;
    } else {
      trendObj[x].trendline.show = false;
    }
  }
  refreshChart();
});
```

10. We reuse the code for the stacked bar chart with revenue by division found in `1168_10_05.html`, but with the new chart we will only show the current division. In our function to format the remote data, we loop through the labels and push each one to `totalDivTicks` as follows:

```
//****** Stacked Product Revenue by Month **********/
var totalDivSeriesObj = [], totalDivTicks = [];

var totalDivDataPull = function(remoteData,options) {
  var i = 0, data = [], divisions = remoteData.divisions;

  $.each(remoteData.labels, function( i, value ) {
    totalDivTicks.push(value);
  });
```

11. Next, we loop through each division, and if it matches the selected division, we populate our data array and our `totalDivSeriesObj` array as follows:

```
$.each( divisions, function( div, obj ) {
  if(selDivision == div) {
    $.each( obj, function( key, value ) {
      data[i] = divisions[div][key];
```

```
            totalDivSeriesObj[i] = { label: key };
            i++;
          });
      }
    });
    return data;
};
```

12. The creation of the plot object and the chart is similar to how we created our charts for the VP dashboard. We can implement this using the following lines of code:

```
var totalDivPlotObj = defaultBarObj(totalDivSeriesObj, $.jqplot.
CategoryAxisRenderer, totalDivDataPull);
  totalDivPlotObj.stackSeries = true;
  totalDivPlotObj.axes.xaxis.ticks = totalDivTicks;
  totalDivPlotObj.legend = { show: true, placement: 'outsideGrid',
location: 'ne' }
  totalDivPlotObj = color_theme(totalDivPlotObj, division_
colors[selDivision]);

  var division_revenue = $.jqplot ('indiv_division_revenue',
'data/12_month_prod_categories.json', totalDivPlotObj);
```

13. For the product returns chart, we start by creating `returnsDataPull` to loop through the labels and the regions to generate our ticks, data, and series data arrays as follows:

```
//****** Product Returns by Region **********/
var returnsSeriesObj = [], returnsTicks = [];

var returnsDataPull = function(remoteData,options) {
  var data = [];

  $.each(remoteData.labels, function(i, value ) {
    returnsTicks.push(value);
  });
  $.each(remoteData.regions, function(key, value ) {
    data.push(value);
    returnsSeriesObj.push( { label: key } );
  });
  return data;
};
```

14. We use the `defaultBarObj` function to build our options for this bar chart. We make it a stacked bar chart, set our ticks, enable the divisional colors, and then create the chart as follows:

```
var returnsPlotObj = defaultBarObj(returnsSeriesObj, $.jqplot.
CategoryAxisRenderer, returnsDataPull);
    returnsPlotObj.stackSeries = true;
    returnsPlotObj.axes.xaxis.ticks = returnsTicks;
    returnsPlotObj = color_theme( returnsPlotObj, company_colors);

    var product_returns = $.jqplot ('division_product_returns',
'data/returns_by_region.json', returnsPlotObj);
```

15. With all of this done, we move to the HTML part of our dashboard. We create links for each division with the respective query string value. When we go into production, passing the value to the JavaScript will be handled on the server side. We also have the h1 tag, as shown in the following code snippet, that is populated when our JavaScript parses the query string:

```
<a href="1168_11_02.html?division=Media-Software">Media-Software</
a> |
<a href="1168_11_02.html?division=Electronics">Electronics</a> |
<a href="1168_11_02.html?division=Nerd_Corral">Nerd Corral</a>
<h1 id="division_name"></h1>
```

16. Like our VP dashboard, we wrap each chart and h2 tag in a `section` tag and add a class as follows:

```
<section class="division_chart">
<h2>Product Revenue by Month</h2>
<div id="indiv_division_revenue" class="w600 h300"></div>
</section>
<section class=" division_chart ">
<h2>Last 12 Months of Product Returns by Region</h2>
<div id="division_product_returns"></div>
</section>
<section class=" division_chart ">
<select id="trendline" name="trendline">
</select>
<h2><span id="division"></span> Product Revenue with Trends</h2>
<div id="division_rev_category" class="w700"></div>
</section>
```

17. We finish by adding style rules to `styles.css`. We float each section to the left and set the minimum width and height. We also change the background color of the legends so when they overlap our charts, we can still read them. This can be implemented as follows:

```
section.division_chart {
  float: left;
  min-width: 48%;
  min-height: 425px;
}

section.division_chart table.jqplot-table-legend {
  background: #fff;
}
```

We load the newly created dashboard in our browser. The two charts showing product revenue use the division colors and the product return chart has the company colors. We switch between the different divisions and see the data and the chart colors change:

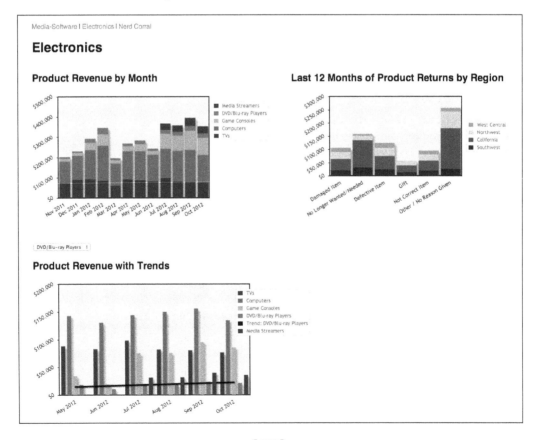

We notice when we select **DVD/Blu-ray Players** from the **Electronics** dashboard drop-down menu, the legend ends up covering some of the chart. This is because we are using the `outside` placement option for our chart. We remember that this option will place the legend outside the div for our chart.

As each chart is wrapped in a `section` tag with a width of 48 percent, this means our legend will move around trying to stay inside the parent container. We could have used `outsideGrid` but that would have shrunk the size of our bar chart, so we made a trade-off.

It is close to lunch time so we decide to go grab something to eat knowing that our meeting will likely be this afternoon. Just as we get to the door, our office phone rings. Calvin tells us we have a meeting to present our dashboards at two o'clock. We hang up and walk down to Calvin's favorite sandwich shop.

Digesting our work

We arrive back in the office a little before two o'clock so we can get everything together for our presentation. Once we're ready, we make our way to the conference room, where Roshan, Sara, and Calvin are waiting on us. Even Jeff from IT has joined us. We connect our laptop and project the VP dashboard on the screen.

"I love it," Sara says after a few moments, "I like how the colors match the company's brand. Also the revenue and profit line chart stands out." Roshan speaks up, "The waterfall chart is nice and with Sara's data, we can see the **Inventory Losses** broken out in the chart below it." I tell them, "We didn't intend it that way. I guess it was a happy accident."

"We also have the divisional dashboard to present," I continue. I remind them that we have mocked up the functionality to change divisions on the chart, at which point you pull up the chart on the projector.

Extending the divisional dashboard

Roshan makes the first comment, "This is great. Maybe in the future we can get the product return data broken out by divisions as well. That way **Electronics** will only see the totals for their division."

Calvin raises his hand. "Is there any way these charts could work as a slideshow? We've got all these TVs around the office we could display them on." Sara jumps in, "I like this idea. It gets relevant information out to more people."

Roshan holds up his hands as if he's trying to slow us down. "We'll need to think it through. We don't want vendors and other non-employees being able to see this data but it's a good idea. However, what we have will work for now."

Dashboard Version 3

"Which brings us to the other two items to discuss," says Roshan. "We have taken baby steps in the area of social media and our daily deals website. We have been tracking social media conversions and want to get this information out there.

We want a chart showing the number of conversions each month and also the monthly revenue as a result of those conversions. We'll leave the rest up to you."

I mention that Roshan said there were two other items. "Right, I'll let Jeff tell you," Roshan says. "Thanks," Jeff says, "We like the charts you created for IT. We're in the process of getting final sign-off on an IT dashboard. Before we move forward, is there any way we can change the donut chart you created? I'm talking about the one showing current browser and version percentages (found in `1168_05_05.html`). We like it, but it would be really nice if we could have a tooltip near the cursor. I'm thinking, since you've used it on other charts, it should be an easy fix."

We tell him we'll look into it. Roshan speaks again, "Well, I think that's everything. We'll check back in later this week."

We get back to the office and start thinking through the social media conversion chart. It would be best to render the revenue data as a bar chart and then we can render the conversions as a line. We can also add a trend line for the revenue.

Since this is going to be the next phase of our dashboards, we begin thinking about things we can add to our chart beyond just the data. We begin reading more on how the `canvas` element works. We come across the Dive Into HTML5 site, `http://diveintohtml5.info/canvas.html`. They discuss how to include images into the canvas. That gets us thinking. What if we added the company logo to the actual chart? Not just overlay it with CSS but make it part of the canvas?

Mixing renderers

With all our ideas fleshed out, we are ready to begin building our chart comparing social media conversions to monthly revenue. We can use the options from our line chart we created for the VP dashboard earlier. We create a new file and begin building our new chart as follows:

1. We start by adding all the necessary plugin files as follows:

```
<script src="../js/jqplot.categoryAxisRenderer.min.js"></script>
```

```
<script src="../js/jqplot.barRenderer.min.js"></script>
<script src="../js/jqplot.canvasTextRenderer.min.js"></script>
<script src="../js/jqplot.canvasAxisTickRenderer.min.js"></script>
<script src="../js/jqplot.canvasAxisLabelRenderer.min.js"></ script>
<script src="../js/jqplot.trendline.min.js"></script>
<script src="../js/functions.js"></script>
<script src="../js/themes.js"></script>
```

2. Next, we create a method to pass back the revenue and conversions from the remote data source. After that we pass in the URL for our remote source to our plot object.

```
<script src="../js/jqplot.canvasAxisLabelRenderer.min.js"></ script>
...
$(document).ready(function(){
  var conversionDataPull = function(remoteData,options) {
    return [remoteData.revenue, remoteData.conversions];
  }

  var conversionRevenue = $.jqplot ('conversionRevenue',
'data/conversion_revenue.json',
    {
```

3. We now paste in the options from our line chart from the VP dashboard. We change the function passed to `dataCallback` under `dataRendererOptions` as follows:

```
grid: {
  backgroundColor: 'rgba(64,0,64,0.25)',
  gridLineColor: '#fff',
  borderColor: '#000',
  shadow: false
},
dataRenderer: remoteDataCallback,
dataRendererOptions: { dataCallback: conversionDataPull },
```

4. We enable smooth lines for our line chart as well as setting `seriesColors` for the bar chart. We also set `axesDefaults` and include `labelRenderer` as follows:

```
seriesDefaults: { rendererOptions: { smooth: true } },
seriesColors: company_colors,
axesDefaults: {
  tickRenderer: $.jqplot.CanvasAxisTickRenderer,
  tickOptions: {
```

```
      angle: -30 ,
      formatString: "$%'d"
   },
   padMax: 1.5,
   labelRenderer: $.jqplot.CanvasAxisLabelRenderer,
   rendererOptions: { alignTicks: true }
},
```

5. We move the revenue series to y2axis and set color, width, and label for
    our trend line. We set the renderer to BarRenderer and set some padding
    and margin for our bars. Next, we set color, width, and label for our
    conversions series. We also enable the legend as follows:

```
series:[
  { label: 'Revenue', yaxis:'y2axis',
    trendline: {
      show: true,
      color: '#DE6FA1',
      lineWidth: 4,
      label: 'Revenue Trend'
    },
    renderer:$.jqplot.BarRenderer,
    rendererOptions: { barMargin: 5, barPadding: 5 }
  },
  { label: 'Conversions',
    lineWidth: 4,
    color: '#9E059E'
  }
],
legend: { show: true, placement: 'outsideGrid'},
```

6. Like our profit and revenue line chart on the VP dashboard, we turn off the
    borders on both our *x* axes. We also set showGridline to false and rotate
    the ticks on the *x* axis as follows:

```
axes:{
  x2axis: { borderWidth: 0 },
  xaxis: {
    renderer:$.jqplot.CategoryAxisRenderer,
    borderWidth: 0,
    tickOptions: {
      formatString: "%b %Y",
      showGridline: false,
      angle: -45
    }
  },
```

7. By setting more options under `axesDefaults`, we only need to change `formatString` for `yaxis` and then set `label` for both *y* axes. We set `padMax` to `1.5` in our defaults because we want to include our logo. We finish our code by calling the `overlayLogo` function to convert the image to a `canvas` element. The function accepts the ID of our chart, a width value, and a location value.

```
      yaxis: {
        label: 'Conversions',
        tickOptions: { formatString: "%'d" }
      },
      y2axis: { label: 'Revenue' }
    }
  });
  overlayLogo('conversionRevenue', 100, 'top');
});
</script>
```

8. We finish the page by adding a headline and the div to contain the chart. To add the logo to the canvas, the logo will need to be accessible from the DOM. We add the image and then add the class `hidden` to hide it when the page loads as follows:

```
<section class="twitter_conversions">
<h2>Revenue from Twitter Conversions</h2>
<div id="conversionRevenue"></div>
</section>
<img src="../images/logo.png" id="company_logo" class="hidden">
```

Before we can load our chart, we need to create the `overlayLogo` function. We want it to reside in `functions.js`.

Adding extra canvas elements

Our `overlayLogo` function will calculate the new height and position for our logo. Then, we will use the `drawImage` method to convert the image and make it part of the main canvas. We wrap all of this in a `setInterval` function because we have to wait for jqPlot to render all the canvas elements before we can add our image. Perform the following steps to add extra canvas elements:

1. We start by setting `yPos` to `bottom` if nothing is passed in for this parameter. When calculating coordinates for a `canvas` element, we begin at the upper-left corner. So, we declare variables for our height and the *x* and *y* coordinates. Next, we create a variable to hold our `setInterval` function as follows:

```
function overlayLogo(id, scaledWidth, yPos) {
  if(typeof(yPos) === 'undefined') { yPos = 'bottom' };
  var height = 0, top = 0, left = 0, canvas = '';
  var checkCanvas = setInterval(function() {
```

2. jqPlot does not add an ID to the `canvas` elements it creates, so we need to locate our `canvas` element using the class name. If the canvas we want exists, we create a new area on the selected canvas to draw our image. Next, we find the DOM element for our logo as follows:

```
canvas = $("#"+id+" .jqplot-event-canvas");
if (canvas.length > 0) {
  var context = canvas[0].getContext("2d");
  var logo = $("#company_logo")[0];
```

3. To get our height, we divide the original height and width to get the ratio and then multiply it by `scaledWidth`. We calculate `left` so that the image is placed five pixels from the right edge of the chart as shown in the following code snippet:

```
height = (logo.height/logo.width) * scaledWidth;
left = canvas[0].width - scaledWidth - 5;
```

4. If `yPos` is set to `bottom`, we calculate the `top` variable so the image will be five pixels from the bottom of the chart. If `yPos` is set to `top`, we place the image at the top edge of the chart as follows:

```
switch (yPos) {
  case 'bottom':
    top = canvas[0].height - height - 5;
    break;
  case 'top':
    top = 0;
    break;
}
```

5. With all our new values, we pass these into the `drawImage` method. Then, we run `clearInterval` so that our interval loop will cease as follows:

```
    context.drawImage(logo, left, top, scaledWidth, height);
    clearInterval(checkCanvas);
  }
}, 100);
}
```

We review the results in our browser and can see the interaction between conversions and revenue. We see that revenue shows an upward trend. The logo also appears in the upper-right corner of our chart. We hope Roshan will appreciate these additions.

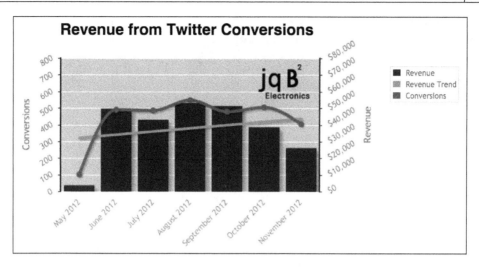

Upon further inspection, we see that the average dollar amount per conversion is $100. However, in October, the average is closer to $125 and in November, it is close to $160. Knowing this, the next step would be to determine what items were sold each month.

With this chart done, it is close to five o'clock so we collect our things and head home. We can look at Jeff's request to add a cursor tooltip to the donut chart in the morning.

Modifying an existing plugin

We arrive in the office the next morning just before nine o'clock. We begin thinking about Jeff's request to add a cursor tooltip to his donut chart. The cursor plugin does not create a tooltip for donut charts. So, if we want a tooltip, we will have to create one. We decide to look at modifying the donut renderer plugin to accomplish this.

We open the file, `jqplot.donutRenderer.js`, found in our `js` folder and save it as a new file called `jqplot.donutRendererV2.js`. We begin working our way through it. The entire plugin is a method attached to the jqPlot object and by default attached to jQuery. We see that `DonutRenderer` inherits its structure from the `LineRenderer` plugin:

```
$.jqplot.DonutRenderer = function(){
    $.jqplot.LineRenderer.call(this);
};

$.jqplot.DonutRenderer.prototype = new $.jqplot.LineRenderer();
$.jqplot.DonutRenderer.prototype.constructor = $.jqplot.
DonutRenderer;
```

We continue moving through the plugin and come to the `init` method, which is where all our options are passed in and set.

1. Since the cursor plugin has an option to show the tooltip, we add one to the properties list for this plugin as follows:

```
// called with scope of a series
$.jqplot.DonutRenderer.prototype.init = function(options, plot)
{
    // Group: Properties
    //
    // prop: diameter
    // Outer diameter of the donut, auto computed by default
    this.diameter = null;
    // prop: innerDiameter
    // Inner diameter of the donut, auto calculated by default.
    // If specified will override thickness value.
    this.innerDiameter = null;
    // prop: showTooltip
    // true to add our custom tooltip.
    this.showTooltip = false;
```

2. We find the `preInit` method where the default renderers for the legend and axes are set, which is done before the chart is created. This gets us thinking. We can inject a div for our tooltip into the chart div. This is what is done for the legend and axes. So at the end of the method, we check to see if the tooltip is enabled and add the div as follows:

```
function preInit(target, data, options) {
    options = options || {};
    ...

    if(options.showTooltip) {
        $("#"+target).append("<div class='jqplot-donut-tooltip'></
div>");
    }
}
```

3. We have a div to hold our tooltip data but we need to find the method that highlights the wedge. We eventually come across the `handleMove` method. Inside the method, we see a reference to the `jqplotDataHighlight` method and the `pageX` and `pageY` variables, which hold our mouse coordinates. Then there is the `highlight` method, which highlights the selected wedge as shown in the following code snippet:

```
function handleMove(ev, gridpos, datapos, neighbor, plot) {
    if (neighbor) {
        ...
```

```
        if (plot.series[ins[0]].highlightMouseOver && !(ins[0] ==
plot.plugins.donutRenderer.highlightedSeriesIndex && ins[1] ==
plot.series[ins[0]]._highlightedPoint)) {
            var evt = jQuery.Event('jqplotDataHighlight');
            evt.which = ev.which;
            evt.pageX = ev.pageX;
            evt.pageY = ev.pageY;
            plot.target.trigger(evt, ins);
            highlight (plot, ins[0], ins[1]);
```

4. We select the `jqplot-donut-tooltip` class within our chart and set the top
   and left properties so it will appear next to our cursor. Once the tooltip is in
   place, we show it as follows:

```
        $(plot.targetId + " .jqplot-donut-tooltip").css({
          top: evt.pageY-50,
          left: evt.pageX
        });
        $(plot.targetId + " .jqplot-donut-tooltip").show();
      }
    }
```

5. In the `else` statement, the wedge is no longer highlighted so we hide the
   tooltip as follows:

```
    else if (neighbor == null) {
      unhighlight (plot);
      $(plot.targetId + " .jqplot-donut-tooltip").hide();
    }
  }
```

We have completed modifying our plugin. Since we are creating custom tooltip data
for our inner ring, we will need to also modify the event handlers in our HTML file.

Modifying our chart to use the cursor tooltip

We open the file, `1168_05_05.html`, and save it as a new file, `1168_11_04.html`.

1. We change the JavaScript file from the old donut plugin file to the new
   donut plugin file. We also include `themes.js` so we can use the company
   colors. Since we are using the company colors, we also get rid of the
   `arrSeriesColors` array as follows:

```
<script src="../js/jqplot.donutRendererV2.js"></script>
<script src="../js/functions.js"></script>
<script src="../js/themes.js"></script>
<script>
var innerRingColors = [];
```

2. With the `parseVersions` function, we switch to use the `company_colors` array as follows:

```
function parseVersions(v,browser) {
  ...
     for (var ver in v[name]) {
       innerRing.push([ver, v[name][ver], name]);
       innerRingColors.push(company_colors[i]);
     }
  ...
  return versions;
}
```

3. Next, after we set `title`, we enable `showTooltip`. We also set `backgroundcolor` and `seriesColors` to the `company_colors` as follows:

```
    title: 'Web Browser Usage',
    showTooltip: true,
    grid: { backgroundColor: $.jqplot.hex2rgb(company_colors[0],
0.1) },
    seriesColors: company_colors,
    seriesDefaults: {
```

4. We finish the changes to our HTML file by changing the selectors to our new tooltip class in the `jqplotDataHighlight` and `jqplotDataUnhighlight` event handlers as follows:

```
      if(seriesIndex == 0) {
        $(".jqplot-donut-tooltip").html(data[0]+' - '+percent.
toFixed(2)+'%');
      } else {
        $(".jqplot-donut-tooltip").html(data[2]+': '+data[0]+' -
'+percent.toFixed(2)+'%');
      }
    }
  );
  $('#purple_browser_usage').on('jqplotDataUnhighlight',
    function (ev, seriesIndex, pointIndex, data) {
      $(".jqplot-donut-tooltip").html('');
    }
  );
```

5. We need to add some CSS styles for our new tooltip. We open `styles.css` and set the positioning and `z-index` so the tooltip will appear next to our cursor and on top of any other layers as follows:

```
#purple_browser_usage .jqplot-donut-tooltip {
```

```
    color: #000;
    position: absolute;
    white-space: nowrap;
    display: none;
    padding: 5px;
    background: rgba(255,255,255,.95);
    border: 1px solid #999;
    border-radius: 5px;
    z-index: 999;
}
```

We load the updated chart and move our cursor around highlighting different wedges. We hover over the wedge for Firefox 26.0.

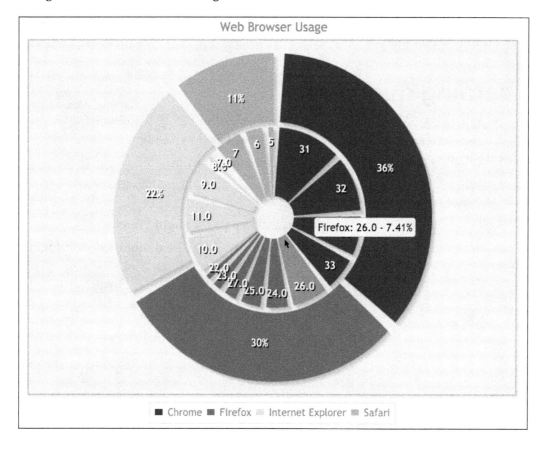

A nice tooltip appears near our cursor. This is a much better option than putting the highlighted data at the top of the chart like before.

It felt a little daunting at first when we began looking through the plugin, but then we began seeing patterns in the structure. We found the methods we needed and accomplished what Jeff asked for.

Later that afternoon, we meet with Roshan, Sara, Jeff, and Calvin. Roshan starts off, "This chart showing conversions is beautiful. I also really like the logo. You know you are going to need to update all the other charts now, right?" Roshan says with a smile.

Jeff speaks up next, "I'm glad you were able to figure out the tooltip issue. I've already got several other ideas for new charts."

With all we have accomplished over the past couple of weeks, we have a good understanding of jqPlot and how we can extend the functionality with plugins. We are confident we can fulfill whatever requests Roshan and the others may send our way during phase three.

Learning questions

1. What JavaScript method did we use to add our logo to the canvas?

2. How can we turn the divisional dashboard into a slideshow?

3. What renderer does the donut renderer inherit from?

4. Where did we add the statement to create the tooltip div within our donut renderer?

5. How did we determine which division's data we should render?

6. What other kind of functionality could we add to the donut renderer plugin?

Summary

In this chapter, we took what we learned from the previous chapters and completed the dashboard projects requested of us. We combined a line chart, waterfall chart, stacked bar chart, and regular bar chart into a dashboard for the vice presidents. Each of these charts work independent of the others and each has its own remote data source. We also created a dashboard for the divisional managers where the data and chart colors change based on which division is selected.

We created a new chart by mixing renderers and also added an image to the chart `canvas` element. Finally, we dug into the code for the donut renderer and modified it to meet our needs.

We covered many of the common options and plugins in jqPlot. Be sure to check out the API documentation at `http://www.jqplot.com/docs/files/jqplot-core-js.html` to find a full list of all the available plugins and options.

With what we have learned, we can get almost any charting project up and running. Along with the technical knowledge of how to create charts, we learned the best use cases for different chart types. This combined understanding of how to build charts and when to use them will help as you begin building charts based on your company's needs.

Answers

Chapter 1, Getting Started

1. The first part is composed of two pieces: the *x* and *y* axes. The other two parts are the grid and the ticks.

2. We can create one object and store it in a variable, and we can use a jQuery selector to create another.

3. In the data series, we set *yaxis* to *y2axis*.

4. The first two options are `outsideGrid` and `insideGrid`. Both of these will place the legend within the plot object. The `outside` option will place the legend outside the object. With this option, the legend may overlap other elements on the page.

5. The four main styles are `circle`, `diamond`, `square`, and x. The other three options are the filled in versions of `circle`, `diamond`, and `square`.

6. We will use $%'d. The dollar sign is literal and the apostrophe tells jqPlot that we want the thousands place separator.

Chapter 2, More Line Charts, Area Charts, and Scatter Plots

1. The first parameter used is `url`. This is the URL of the remote data source. The next parameter is `plot`, which is a copy of the jqPlot object we created. The final parameter is `options`, which is a hash of options we can pass in.

2. JSONP runs asynchronously and jqPlot runs synchronously. jqPlot will finish building the chart before the data is returned and will, therefore, not have any data displayed.

3. We pass the name of the function used to retrieve our remote data.

4. We need to rank our data series from largest to smallest so that the largest ones do not cover all the other series.

5. For whatever series we want to show a trend line for, we will create a `trendline` property and set the `show` property to `true`.

Chapter 3, Bar Charts and Digging into Data

1. If we wish to enable labels for all our series under `seriesDefaults`, we will add the `pointLabels: { show: true }` property. If we only want to do this for one series, we will find that element in our `series` array and set `show` to `true` under `pointsLabels`.

2. To rotate your tick labels, you will need to enable `canvasAxisTickRenderer` in your plot. This plugin is dependent on `canvasTextRenderer`, so you will need to include this file as well.

3. By setting `shadowAlpha` close to `1.0`, the shadow on the bar will appear more like the side of the bar than a shadow. This gives the bar a three-dimensional look.

4. By using a trend line, we demonstrated that revenue for a particular category was increasing or decreasing over time.

5. We bound an event to `jqplotDataHighlight` so that more data appeared when a user hovered over an area. When a user moved away from that area, we bound an event to `jqplotDataUnhighlight` to make the data disappear.

6. There are two ways. First, we can break up each regional amount and group it by return reason. So, we will have four bars corresponding to each region for **Damaged Item**, and so on. The other way is to group the six reasons under each region. So, we will have a bar for **Damaged Item** through **Other | No Reason Given** under **Southwest**, and so on.

7. Knowing what products were returned can be helpful. If one brand of TV accounted for 75 percent of the **Defective Item** or **Damaged Item** categories, it will be very useful. If you have data showing a small group of employees were the ones giving out most of the returns, action can be taken.

Chapter 4, Horizontal and Stacked Bar Charts

1. We need to switch their order from `[[x, y], [x, y], [x, y]]` to `[[y, x], [y, x], [y, x]]`.

2. We use the `canvasOverlay` option to create a horizontal or vertical line. Within this property, we must set `show` to `true` and create an `objects` array that holds the options for each line we will create.

3. Under `tickOptions`, set `showGridline` to `false` for the axis you want to remove grid lines from. If you want to remove both the grid lines and the ticks, you can set `show` to `false` under `tickOptions`.

4. Within the `series` array, you will need to create a property called `pointLabels`. Within this object, you pass an array to the `label` property. It is expected that there will be a label for each data point in the series.

5. There are two main limitations of both charts. If there are too many data points and we keep the chart at a manageable size, the bars will be too small to see. If we increase the size of the chart to accommodate all the bars, the user will have to scroll back and forth, and this will make data comparison difficult.

Chapter 5, Pie Charts and Donut Charts

1. We passed an array of color values to `seriesColors` to override the default colors in jqPlot.

2. We can set `dataLabelNudge` under `rendererOptions` for a series to move the labels further from the center of the pie.

3. If we do not set a value for `dataLabels`, the label will default to showing the percentage of the wedge. The other two options are `label`, which is the value passed in as the x value, and `value`, which is the number passed in as the y value.

4. We set `numberRows` to `1` under `rendererOptions` for our legend.

5. If there are a lot of small wedges, it will be hard to tell what category they belong to or compare them to other categories. Also, you cannot determine trends from a pie chart.

6. When a user clicks on a wedge showing browser usage, it can load a second pie chart showing the versions.

7. We will start by looping through each division and storing the data in a temporary array. We will then sort the data and add it to the data array getting returned from our `dataPull` function. We will also set `seriesColors` to match the divisional colors used in the three pie charts.

Chapter 6, Spice Up Your Charts with Animation, Tooltips, and Highlighting

1. The hierarchy begins with `rendererOptions` followed by the `animation` property. Within the `animation` property, we set the `speed` attribute.

2. Under the `cursor` option, we must set `showVerticalLine` to true in order for the cursor to display values in the legend.

3. The tooltip can be placed in the eight compass directions of n, ne, e, se, s, sw, w, and nw. In conjunction with the directional placements, the cursor can remain static in the specified location or it can follow the cursor.

4. You can set `tooltipAxes` to x, y, xy, both (which is an alias for xy), or yx. This option determines which values are used and in what order they are passed to the highlighter plugin.

Chapter 7, Stock Market Charts – OHLC and Candlestick Charts

1. OHLC stands for open, high, low, close.

2. A candlestick chart is composed of the body and the shadow. The shadow extending from the top of the body is called the wick, and the shadow extending from the bottom of the body is called the tail.

3. In order to skip a value, we need to pass in the position of each value in the data array. For our OHLC chart, we have five values: date, opening price, high price, low price, and closing price. The date is in position 1, while the closing price is in position 5. If we want to show the opening price and the closing price separated by a line break, we will format our string as `%2$.2f<br>%5$.2f`.

4. The cursor plugin contains the zoom functionality.

5. The first option is `fillUpBody` and it needs to be set to true. This will cause all our candlesticks to be colored. Next, we set `upBodyColor` and `downBodyColor` to the colors we choose to represent prices that closed higher and lower than the opening price.

6. If there is a stock split, it will be good to represent on the chart. A company buyout or merger will also be relevant. Really, any news that contributes to large movements of the stock will be useful.

7. The date values for a canvas overlay line need to be converted to an epoch timestamp, which is the number of seconds since January 1, 1970.

8. Revenue and profit will be the most obvious choices. However, there are many other options. We can graph out our expenses. We can also represent the market share of our competitors to find correlations with our stock price.

Chapter 8, Bubble Charts, Block Plots, and Waterfalls

1. We will set `varyBarColor` to `true` to have each bar colored differently.

2. We pass in a second `y` value, which is used to calculate the radius of our bubble. The fourth value in our data array is either a label or an object containing the label and an optional color.

3. For the `formatString` option, we need to set the value to `%'.2f` so that our chart will display the number to two decimal places.

4. These two charts are similar to scatterplots.

5. We used the Enhanced Legend plugin to turn off the series in our block plot.

6. We can show how each division contributes to the overall revenue. We can also show the interaction of inventory buying against the budget along with the costs of the various product loss categories.

Chapter 9, Showing Real-time Data with Our Charts

1. The `redraw` method is used when we want to manually update plot data or change properties in our chart. If we want to change the axes or have jqPlot update the data series from a remote data source, we need to use `replot`.

2. The axes and ticks were rendered before the data from our remote source was processed.

3. If too many data series are added to the remote data source, the charts generated will be unreadable.

4. We set the `min` and `max` values for our gauge. We created `label` and used `labelPosition` to move the label below the chart. We created an array for the `ticks` option to allow us know the position of where our needle sat. We also set `intervals` to create colored bands below the needle and used `intervalColors` to color those bands.

5. We can overload jqPlot with the amount of data it will need to process and try to plot. Also, with too many data points, the chart will be unreadable.

Chapter 10, Beautifying and Extending Your Charts

1. Function expression is the term used to describe storing a function in a variable.

2. DRY stands for "don't repeat yourself".

3. The only styling we can do with CSS on a `canvas` element is hide it or change its positioning on the page.

4. The first level will be `seriesColors`. If we want to override any of the colors in this array, we can set the `color` property for the individual series in the `series` array.

5. We can create include files for the different charts we want to create. These files will include all the script tags that add the various plugins to the HTML. We can also modify our `dataPull` functions so that based on options passed in through `dataRendererOptions`, we can reuse the same method multiple times.

Chapter 11, Bringing it All Together

1. We used `drawImage`, which is part of the `getContext` method available in the HTML `canvas` element.

2. We can use a plugin that will move the container divs off the screen. We can also hide or show the slides using animations so that they appear to fade in and out. If we change options of our chart while it is hidden, we will need to run `replot` after the plot is shown.

3. It inherits from the line renderer.

4. We created our tooltip div within the `preInit` method.

5. We used a query string value to determine which division's data to render.

6. We could create a line from the middle of the donut to the highlighted wedge using the canvas elements and include the tooltip data in the middle. We could create a method to determine the best color to use for each data label based on the method that generates the highlight colors.

Index

M

meter gauge chart
  creating, with Wi-Fi users 156-158
  refreshing, from remote data 158, 159
multiple data series
  adding 14, 15
  multiple y axes, adding 15, 16
  used, for creating bar chart 51-53
multiple y axes
  adding, on multiple data series 15, 16

N

negative colors
  setting, on bar chart 178-180

O

OAuth
  URL 27
objects
  used, for combining chart 183, 184
OHLC chart
  about 120
  building, with previous
      quarter's data 122-125
outsideGrid option 17
outside option 18
overlayLogo function 205

P

padMax option, bar chart 50
padMin option, bar chart 50
pad option, bar chart 50
parseBrowsers function 99
parseVersions function 99
pie chart
  building, with empty wedges 91-94
  creating, with multiple data points 86-89
  creating, with product category revenue 94
  donut chart 97
  functionality, adding 90, 91
  limitations 85, 86
  styling 90, 91

product category
  trend lines, adding to 54-58

R

remote data array
  values, adding 133-135
remote datasets
  modifying, with replot method 160-164
remote data sources
  project's scope, adding 27
  working with 24-27
renderers
  mixing 202-205
replot method
  used, for building chart
      dynamically 164-169
  used, for modifying remote
      datasets 160-164
reusable plot objects
  creating 180-182

S

scatterplot charts (scatter charts)
  about 39
  creating 40-42
second xaxis
  using 176-178
Social Media Shares chart 112
shadows, candlestick chart 121
stacked area charts
  about 29
  creating, with revenue 32-34
  event handler, adding to 63-66
stacked bar chart
  limits 76
  using 73-76

T

tail, candlestick chart 121
tooltip
  adding, to canvas overlay lines 131-133
  following, cursor 107, 108

Thank you for buying

Learning jqPlot

About Packt Publishing

Packt, pronounced 'packed', published its first book "*Mastering phpMyAdmin for Effective MySQL Management*" in April 2004 and subsequently continued to specialize in publishing highly focused books on specific technologies and solutions.

Our books and publications share the experiences of your fellow IT professionals in adapting and customizing today's systems, applications, and frameworks. Our solution based books give you the knowledge and power to customize the software and technologies you're using to get the job done. Packt books are more specific and less general than the IT books you have seen in the past. Our unique business model allows us to bring you more focused information, giving you more of what you need to know, and less of what you don't.

Packt is a modern, yet unique publishing company, which focuses on producing quality, cutting-edge books for communities of developers, administrators, and newbies alike. For more information, please visit our website: www.packtpub.com.

About Packt Open Source

In 2010, Packt launched two new brands, Packt Open Source and Packt Enterprise, in order to continue its focus on specialization. This book is part of the Packt Open Source brand, home to books published on software built around Open Source licenses, and offering information to anybody from advanced developers to budding web designers. The Open Source brand also runs Packt's Open Source Royalty Scheme, by which Packt gives a royalty to each Open Source project about whose software a book is sold.

Writing for Packt

We welcome all inquiries from people who are interested in authoring. Book proposals should be sent to author@packtpub.com. If your book idea is still at an early stage and you would like to discuss it first before writing a formal book proposal, contact us; one of our commissioning editors will get in touch with you.

We're not just looking for published authors; if you have strong technical skills but no writing experience, our experienced editors can help you develop a writing career, or simply get some additional reward for your expertise.

Tableau Data Visualization Cookbook

ISBN: 978-1-84968-978-6   Paperback: 172 pages

Over 70 recipes for creating visual stories with your data using Tableau

1. Quickly create impressive and effective graphics that would usually take hours in other tools.

2. Lots of illustrations to keep you on track.

3. Includes examples that apply to a general audience.

Python Data Visualization Cookbook

ISBN: 978-1-78216-336-7   Paperback: 280 pages

Over 60 recipes that will enable you to learn how to create attractive visualizations using Python's most popular libraries

1. Learn how to set up an optimal Python environment for data visualization.

2. Understand the topics such as importing data for visualization and formatting data for visualization.

3. Understand the underlying data and how to use the right visualizations.

Please check **www.PacktPub.com** for information on our titles

open source
community experience distilled

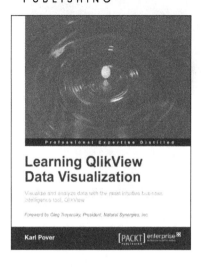

Learning QlikView Data Visualization

Learning QlikView Data Visualization

Visualize and analyze data with the most intuitive business intelligence tool, QlikView

Foreword by Oleg Troyansky, President, Natural Synergies, Inc.

Karl Pover

[PACKT] enterprise

Learning QlikView Data Visualization

ISBN: 978-1-78217-989-4   Paperback: 156 pages

Visualize and analyze data with the most intuitive business intelligence tool, QlikView

1. Explore the basics of data discovery with QlikView.

2. Perform rank, trend, multivariate, distribution, correlation, geographical, and what-if analysis.

3. Deploy data visualization best practices for bar, line, scatterplot, heat map, tables, histogram, box plot, and geographical charts.

4. Communicate and monitor data using a dashboard.

Social Data Visualization with HTML5 and JavaScript

Social Data Visualization with HTML5 and JavaScript

Leverage the power of HTML5 and JavaScript to build compelling visualizations of social data from Twitter, Facebook, and more

Simon Timms

PACKT open source

Social Data Visualization with HTML5 and JavaScript

ISBN: 978-1-78216-654-2   Paperback: 104 pages

Leverage the power of HTML5 and JavaScript to build compelling visualizations of social data from Twitter, Facebook, and more

1. Learn how to use JavaScript to create compelling visualizations of social data.

2. Use the d3 library to create impressive SVGs.

3. Master OAuth and how to authenticate with social media sites.

Please check **www.PacktPub.com** for information on our titles

www.ingramcontent.com/pod-product-compliance
Lightning Source LLC
Chambersburg PA
CBHW060546060326
40690CB00017B/3619